新时代
英语技能大赛
实训与指导

林冰洁　李婷婷　王诗媛◎主编

ENGLISH SKILLS
COMPETITON
PRACTICE & GUIDANCE

浙江工商大學出版社
ZHEJIANG GONGSHANG UNIVERSITY PRESS
· 杭州 ·

图书在版编目(CIP)数据

新时代英语技能大赛实训与指导 / 林冰洁, 李婷婷,
王诗媛主编. — 杭州 : 浙江工商大学出版社, 2022.6
　　ISBN 978-7-5178-4745-8

　　Ⅰ. ①新… Ⅱ. ①林… ②李… ③王… Ⅲ. ①英语课
—中等专业学校—教学参考资料 Ⅳ. ①G634.413

　　中国版本图书馆 CIP 数据核字(2021)第239726号

新时代英语技能大赛实训与指导
XINSHIDAI YINGYU JINENG DASAI SHIXUN YU ZHIDAO
林冰洁　李婷婷　王诗媛 主编

责任编辑	柳　河	
责任校对	李远东	
封面设计	沈　婷	
责任印制	包建辉	
出版发行	浙江工商大学出版社	
	（杭州市教工路198号　邮政编码310012）	
	（E-mail:zjgsupress@163.com）	
	（网址:http://www.zjgsupress.com）	
	电话:0571-88904980,88831806(传真)	
排　　版	杭州朝曦图文设计有限公司	
印　　刷	浙江全能工艺美术印刷有限公司	
开　　本	889mm×1194mm　1/16	
印　　张	7	
字　　数	262千	
版 印 次	2022年6月第1版　2022年6月第1次印刷	
书　　号	ISBN 978-7-5178-4745-8	
定　　价	30.00元	

编委会

主　编　　林冰洁　李婷婷　王诗媛

编　委　　邱　盛　徐　帆　王婉宇

目录

第一章 大赛详情

第一节 赛事介绍与解析

一、赛事介绍

宁波市中职学生英语职业技能竞赛（旅游英语、商贸英语）基于教育部《中等职业学校英语教学大纲》的课程任务和教学目标，旨在培养学生在日常生活和职业场景中的英语应用能力。该竞赛通过"以赛促学、以赛促教"的方式，令学生初步养成职场英语的应用能力，提高教师的教学应用能力，并为全国职业院校技能大赛（简称："国赛"）中职组职业英语技能赛项储备人才。

自2018年起，宁波市中职学生英语职业技能竞赛取消原有的两个组别，即服务类和其他类，新增旅游英语和商贸英语两个组别。同时，赛项也从4个环节变为2个环节。每个组别的参赛队以校组队，每队有2名选手和2名指导教师。每校可以兼报两个组别，每名选手只能报一个组别。调整后的2个赛项环节分别为"英语基本技能测评"和"主题产品营销"。

"英语基本技能测评"是上机笔试环节，限时1小时，满分40分。该环节测试形式和测试内容与以往国赛的第一个环节"在线测评"类似，考查职业场景下的英语专业基本能力。该环节得分计2位参赛选手平均分的40%入总分。

"主题产品营销"是宁波市中职学生英语职业技能竞赛的预报国赛方案，满分60分。两名参赛选手以团队形式，分A、B角色参加竞赛。A选手以企业主要经营或管理者身份，根据赛前2周公布的题目，分析目标客户群体，进行资料搜集和讲稿准备，在2分钟内用英语对相关产品或服务进行口头推介（40分）；B选手在现场与提问嘉宾就主题产品或服务以及相关专业知识进行90秒（包括提问时间）的互动问答（20分）。

二、赛事解析

（一）概况

"主题产品营销"环节的设计以英语学科课程标准为参考，以核心素养为依托，从主题产品入手，令选手充分运用职场语言进行营销。向中外客户营销的过程能够展现选手跨文化感知和理解中外思维差异的能力。公布赛题之后的两周准备时间里，选手可充分发挥其自主学习能力收集资料、撰稿修改。A、B选手互助参赛的比赛形式来源于国赛第二环节和第三环节——"情景交际"和"职场应用"。和国赛的两个环节相比，"主题产品营销"环节中，A选手有充足的时间准备，完成资料搜集、撰稿、脱稿演讲等步骤。A选手讲演时间相对较长，因而挑选选手时，应优先考虑语音条件好的学生，以语音洪量，音色悦耳，发音准确，能合理运用连读、重音、停顿、升降调等演讲技巧，台风稳健，笔试成绩突出且发挥稳定为考量标准。在进行营销时，A选手要注意亲和力、感染力、舞台张力，令讲述更加生动，引人入胜。B选手则需根据问题进行现场回答，因此B选手应具备优秀的听力理解能力及较强的逻辑思维能力、反应能力和语言组织能力。进行"主题产品营销"环节时，A选手要动之以情，B选手要晓之以理，二人配合默契，方能使产品得到广大评委的青睐。

与国赛两大组别不同，宁波市中职学生英语职业技能竞赛分为旅游服务类和财经商贸类两个组别。它们是对国赛服务类组别的细化。竞赛虽然考查的是学生中职英语技能方面的能力，但这两年的改革实则弱化了因为即时性因素而强化的英语能力考查，而更重视学生在涉外旅游、商业贸易上的职业意识，以及对相关行业的理解和职业操守。学生的表现要"知行合一"，符合社会主义核心价值观。

此外，赛项用时缩短，评委注意力更集中，比赛因提前的充分准备增加了可观赏性，也缩小了各组之间语言实力的差距。所以，以商贸类组别为例，"主题产品营销"环节的设置符合教育部《中等职业学校商品经营专业教学标准》中使用沟通技巧拉近与顾客间的距离，推介商品，促成交易的要求。就旅游服务类而言，两位选手除了需要增进英语技能外，还需要了解、理解、掌握和应用服务礼仪，了解和理解饭店服务、管理和旅游文化。尤其在服务礼仪方面，两名选手和指导老师要掌握服务意识的基本概念和知识，培养社交能力，提升言谈技巧、导游服务礼仪、涉外礼宾服务以及礼仪危机处理方面的知识与技巧。

同时，指导老师应注意国家的政策导向和与教育相关的时事新闻，在竞赛训练和了解专家出题意图上有大致方向和把握。例如，2019年，中职新增了46个专业，在财经商贸类中增加了跨境电子商务、网络营销等以服务"一带一路"建设，适应新零售、无人零售、线上线下融合发展的新态势；在旅游服务类中新增了康养休闲旅游服务等专业以适应生态旅游、文化旅游、休闲旅游、山地旅游发展的新趋势和生活休闲、文化娱乐服务行业的大发展。

专业类	专业名称	专业（技能）方向举例	专业类	专业名称	专业（技能）方向举例
财经商贸类	跨境电子商务	—	旅游服务类	康养休闲旅游服务	康养旅游服务
	移动商务	—			休闲旅游服务
	网络营销	—		中西面点	中式面点制作
	商务阿拉伯语、商务泰语	—			西式面点制作
	冷链物流服务与管理	冷藏与生鲜加工		茶艺与茶营销	茶艺服务与管理
		冷链配送服务			茶营销与管理
	国际货运代理	—			茶道养生

虽然确切的评分细则并未公布，每年的评判侧重也略有不同，但通过对以往国赛的观察分析，以及参加这两年"新时期"的技能大赛、市赛所积累的经验，我们不难发现，评委旨在考查参赛选手的综合语言应用能力及基本职业素养。其中，就英语能力方面，主要考查A选手观点表达是否明确，条理是否清晰，表述是否自然且符合相关职业特点，占分约40%；考查B选手是否能准确理解信息和正确回答问题，陈述是否全面，条理是否清晰，理由是否充分，以及在表述中所体现出来的职业自信和稳健台风的综合表现，占分约20%。

（二）解题思路与注意事项

不论商贸类还是旅游类，A选手的讲演要切题，主题应别具一格、与众不同，给人耳目一新的感觉。所以，A选手撰稿和演讲都应强化自己的主题，让评委在讲演结束后有余音绕梁、念念不忘之感。B选手互动问答部分的题目并不会提前公布，所以指导老师可根据学生讲演的主题和专业特点进行预测押题，并让学生不断演练，做到万无一失。

以2019年旅游组进行举例分析。

原题

Background

A delegation of 5 members from New Zealand are attending a six-day long business meeting in Beijing. They have a very tight schedule and only have a day's break. They love Chinese culture such as the architecture, food, arts and have great interest in Chinese history. So they want to take the chance and have a one-day tour in China. Since most of them have been to Beijing before, they prefer a tour outside Beijing. They also want to experience the high-speed train in China. The following is their simple memo in Beijing.

Date	Time	Things to do
DEC. 15	09:00—12:00 14:00—18:00	At the meeting the whole day
DEC. 16	09:00—12:00 14:00—18:00	At the meeting the whole day
DEC. 17	09:00—12:00 14:00—15:00	At the meeting the whole morning Free after 3 o'clock in the afternoon
DEC. 18		Free the whole day
DEC. 19	08:30—12:00 14:00—18:00	At the meeting the whole day (There is a very important seminar in the morning, and they will deliver a speech.)
DEC. 20	09:00—12:00 14:00—18:00	At the meeting the whole day

Task

Suppose you are their tour guide. Design a one-day tour plan for them and give an oral introduction to the highlights of the day.

Requirements

- You should first choose an appropriate destination for them in China.
- The tour plan must be practical and achievable in real-world situations.
- The introduction must be given in English.
- You have two minutes to deliver your introduction.
- You can and can only use static images(静态图片) as multi-media aids for your introduction.

现场互动(B选手)Questions：

1. Can you tell me 3 reasons for choosing this destination?

2. What measures will you take if we miss the train?

注意事项

要领千万条,清楚审题第一条。首先,主题营销任务是 Design a one-day tour plan,即"一日游",也就是以北京为中心,辐射一天可来回且还可旅游的地点。挑选地点时,选手要考虑当地的旅游特色和历史文化,避免与他人重复的可能性。2019年的竞赛中,多组参赛队均挑选天津为旅游目的地,所以在具体景点挑选和文化挖掘时,较大程度上与其他参赛队重合。高度的重复率容易产生听觉、视觉疲劳,难抓眼球。

明确地点后,在制订旅游路线时,选手应考虑中国的传统文化,设计有深度,有趣味的主题,比如探索唐诗之美,体验汉字文化、木工技艺,挖掘饮食文化等,同时,选手也需要注意所涉及活动的连贯性。

此外,参加技能大赛演讲,选手的服装要符合主题营销和场合的正式原则,不着奇装异服,以符合职场和学生身份的服装进行主题营销。

B选手回答问题时要注意合理分配时间,回答不要过于简单,要给出合理的回答,并给出2—3个理由进行论证、解释。由于答题过程中并不提示时间,所以选手回答第一道题的时间应尽量压缩,以保证第二道题的发挥时间。一般来说,一道题大概8—10个句子,时间控制在40秒以内。平时训练时就需要掐时以养成计时好习惯,增加学生对40秒时长的感知度,这样学生能更好地在比赛中控制自己的应答时间。B选手的回答应表现自然、有理有据,减少背诵的感觉,"骗"过评委的耳朵。针对2019年的互动问答的第二题,B选手应结合专业知识,做出解释和弥补的方案,如改换下班列车,修改行程,给出错过火车的原因并提供一定补偿等。值得注意的是,选手应明确旅游业是服务行业,经营者、服务人员的态度尤为重要。诚恳、认真、关切的品质是游客非常重视的,所以,应对上述问题的第一步是对发生的特殊情况表示抱歉,尔后,再开展一系列补救措施。

"台上一分钟,台下十年功。"A、B选手在"主题产品营销"环节所要展现的语言技能、职业素养、舞台风采、竞赛水平都需要通过素日里的稳扎稳打和定向训练来提高。只有下功夫,才能在比赛场上信手拈来,应付自如。

第二节 笔试原题展示

本环节以2017年全国职业院校技能大赛"在线测评"的原题为例,简要解析试题要求、解题技巧以及备赛要点,帮助读者了解题型,做好赛前准备。

"在线测评"分为听力和阅读两个部分,评估学生在通用生活和职业场景下的英语应用能力。本环节题型多样,有单项选择、补全信息、图文匹配、完形填空等多种形式;难度适中,适合中职阶段英语水平较高的学生,少有偏题、怪题;切合实际,与现实生活联系密切,反映职场中的真实情境。在备赛时,学生需要熟悉各类题型,掌握生活场景、职业应用等相关词汇和表达方式,做到心中有数,并不断强化英语听力、阅读能力。

一、Part I Listening 听力(40%)

(一)Task 1 Listen and choose

在本节中,选手将听到10个句子和相应的问题,每道题配有 A、B、C 三幅图片,选手应选择与题目内容相符合的一幅图片。每道题读两遍。每题有 10 秒钟的作答时间。

考题主要考查选手对生活场景、地标建筑、职业名称、体育项目和交通工具等语言场景的掌握程度。选手需要在日常生活中对相应词汇有一定的积累并具备对应的文化知识,例如能正确区分tennis和golf(见例1),了解牛排steak的发音,知道"塔桥"是伦敦的地标建筑以及掌握必要的飞机、高铁等交通场景中所用到的单词和词组。教师在培训过程中需要涉及不同领域的知识和文化,辅导学生掌握该场景中一些较为重要的表达,例如"系好安全带""飞机即将起飞""禁止吸烟"等。此外,学生也要多进行听力训练。

例1：

6. (　　)

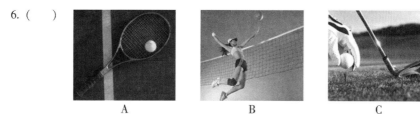

A　　　　　　　B　　　　　　　C

（二）Task 2　Listen and match

在本节中，选手将听到一段较长的对话。选手要根据对话内容匹配信息并将与信息对应的字母填写在表格中。该题有两条冗余信息。对话读两遍。选手有 1 分钟的作答时间。

该题以考查学生词汇基础为目的，以听力的形式让学生正确选择不同学生喜爱的课程。在日常生活中，选手要针对几个常见的主题，例如体育、餐饮、交通、学习等进行词汇的学习和背诵，并能熟练运用。该题考查的是选手对于不同课程名称的敏感性，涉及相应的词汇可分为简单型（例如艺术、音乐和体育领域的）以及困难型（例如化学、物理和生物领域的）。针对这样的题型，日常词汇背诵是选手夯实基础的第一步。在此基础上，选手还需要多多涉猎不同的领域，掌握服务型场景的句型和表达并加强听力练习。

例2：

Example:	0. Peter	A		A	Chemistry
	11. Carol			B	Art
	12. Emily			C	Music
	13. Ben			D	Language
	14. Mark			E	Physics
	15. Martin			F	Math
				G	PE
				H	Biology

（三）Task 3　Listen and write

在本节中，选手将听到一段较长的对话并根据对话内容填空。对话读两遍。选手有 1 分钟的作答时间。

本节是听力考试中难度较高的一部分。相比之前的选择题，本题需要选手在听辨的基础上进行书写，这给选手增大了考试难度。根据题目给出的一部分信息，选手需要填充相应缺失的内容，例如 XX 14th 和 XX years old（见例3）。根据相应的提示，我们可以推断出 14th 之前缺失的是月份，而其词性是名词，而年龄之前缺的是数字。对于此类题目，选手要养成对该类信息的易感性，同时习惯通过推断空格内我们需要填的单词的词性来提高正确率。

例3：

Dete of the flight:	16. _____ 14th
Age of the man's daughter:	17. _____ years old

二、Part II　Reading　阅读（60%）

（一）Task 1　Read and choose

本节有6条描述和7幅图片。选手需要将这些描述与相应的图片匹配起来,其中有一幅多余的图片需要选手甄别。

本节主要考查选手理解描述性语句的能力。选手要读懂每一条对物品的描述,分辨其中的差别,并选择相应的图片。描述中可能出现生词,造成理解障碍,故选手应善于捕捉关键词,例如例4中的第22题,只要能锁定关键信息measure distances即可破题。此外,本节中出现的物品、词语均属同类(文具类),故选手在备考时应注意分门别类地背诵单词,做到系统性地掌握。

例4:

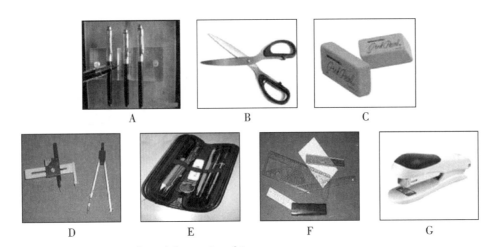

Example: 0. ＿＿＿＿＿ It is a tool used for cutting things.

21. ＿＿＿＿＿ It is a device used to apply ink to a surface, usually paper, for writing or drawing.

22. ＿＿＿＿＿ It is an instrument used in geometry, technical drawing, printing and engineering to measure distances.

（二）Task 2　Read and choose

本节有4个文本和6个问题。选手需要将这些文本与相应的问题匹配起来,并把与文本对应的字母填写在表格中。

本节主要考查学生阅读策略运用,尤其是扫读(scanning)和对不同文体的理解能力。选手需要逐一阅读问题,明确需要寻找的信息,然后快速扫读4个文本,确定提供对应信息的文本。在找寻正确的文本信息时,选手应根据文体,先做大致判断,缩小搜寻范围,例如例5中的第26题,关键信息为job requirements,四篇文体分别为"电子邮件""招聘启事""备忘录""邮件/信件"。选手先迅速预测"招聘启事"是最有可能的关联信息,再进行扫读即可锁定目标。

例5:

Which text telles you:

Example:	0. the name of Jim's friend?	A
	26. the requirements for the part-time job?	

（三）Task 3　Read and choose

本节有6段描述和7条相关的信息。选手需要将这些描述和相应的信息匹配起来,并把与信息对应的字母填写在横线上,其中有一个多余的信息需要选手甄别。

本节主要考查选手理解描述性语句的能力,以及相应生活常识的掌握情况。选手需要快速看一遍选项,对其类型做到心中有数,再逐一阅读每条描述,提取关键信息,找到对应的选项(见例6)。以例6为例,学生在阅读后即可发现关键信息为exchange some US dollars,故应选bank。此外,例题中的选项均为同类型词语,备考时选手应注意掌握。如不认识备选的单词,则无从下手。

例6:

Public services offered in the community

A. the post office　　　B. the bank　　　C. the cinema　　　　D. the gym

E. the clinic　　　　F. Jinghai Training School　　　G. the supermarket

Lucy is a sales manager of BBC. She will go on a business trip in Canada. _____ She is going to exchange some US dollars.

(四)Task 4　Read and choose

本节有两篇短文,每篇5个问题,要求选手从每题所给的A、B、C三个选项中选出最佳答案。

本节主要考查选手阅读篇章、了解文章大意以及捕捉细节的能力,属于常规型阅读。此类题型的解题步骤通常为"通读全文——阅读题目——找出关键信息、定位词——阅读相关语句——比较选项,确定答案"。此类题型要求选手仔细、耐心,紧贴文本寻找答案,避免想当然或过度解读。

(五)Task 5　Read and choose

本节有一篇短文,其中分设10个空,每个空有A、B、C三个选项。选手需要从中选出最佳答案,将文章补充完整。

本节主要考查选手联系前后文、补全信息的能力,同时强调对语法、词语搭配的熟练应用。选手需要在理解文章大意的基础上,对缺失信息进行合理推测,并在三个选项中选出最符合文章逻辑、语法规则的选项,使得文章完整、表意准确。本节中既有对词性的辨析(如第46题)、对词组搭配的考查(如第48题),有对文章情境理解的考查(如第49题),也有对语法规则的考查(如第50题)。本节对学生能力要求较高。

例7:

Hi, Tina,

Thanks for writing. You asked me about my job, so I'll tell you something about it. After graduation from a medical vocational school, I found my first job last year. Its title is Emergency Medical Technician.

It is a ____46____ job. While you are working, you must be ready for a ____47____ emergency at any moment. I'll ____48____ you an example. Last night when we were having dinner, we got ____49____ about a serious car accident. A ____50____ girl was badly hurt. She was bleeding ____51____ when we arrived. I stopped the bleeding and drove her to the hospital as soon as possible. I probably ____52____ her life. Although the pay isn't very ____53____, I love this job. It is a great one. It's nice to know that I'm helping people. ____54____, I'm happy I'm putting what I've learned into ____55____.

(　　)46. A. stressful　　　　　B. stressed　　　　　C. stressfully

(　　)47. A. terrible　　　　　B. wonderful　　　　　C. terrific

(　　)48. A. take　　　　　　B. have　　　　　　C. give

( )49. A. an invitation   B. a call   C. a letter

( )50. A six year old   B. six-years-old   C. six-year-old

第三节 "主题产品营销"环节原题展示

本节,我们以"先按年份再分组别"的编排方式展示宁波市中职英语技能大赛2018年、2019年的第二环节,即"主题产品营销"的真题。参考文章是凝结编者团队智慧结晶的相关产品介绍(A选手部分,B选手部分在本书后面章节再详细展开)。值得一提的是,编者团队所给出的参考文章是经过"真金火炼""真枪实弹"的检验,在赛场上拿到高分的作品,有一定的参考价值。

一、2018年

(一)商贸类

Background

Air pollution is a major environmental risk to health. It is often referred to as "the silent killer". A World Health Organization report in 2016 estimates that around 7 million people die every year from outdoor and indoor air pollution.

In China, the public concern about air pollution and related health risk has been rising in recent years. A lot of people consider it a big problem. While the government is taking action to handle the challenge, ordinary people are also looking for ways to protect themselves and their family from the polluted air. This opens up business opportunities for some companies.

Task

Suppose you are a marketing professional of a company. Your company provides products or services which can protect ordinary people from air pollution. Choose one of such products or services and give a presentation to promote it to English-speaking foreigners living in China.

Requirements

• The product or service you choose must be practical and achievable in real-world situations.

• The presentation must be given in English.

• You have two minutes to deliver your presentation.

• You can and can only use static images(静态图片) as multi-media aids for your presentation.

【参考文章】

Ladies and gentlemen, I am Tia, the Marketing Director from FIT Corporation and this is my colleague Jack, Director of R&D.

Nowadays, air pollution emerges as the top health hazard around the world. The degraded air quality is claiming over 7 million human lives each year and is breeding illnesses like coughing, asthma, and worsening conditions of hearts and lungs.

To address this urgent and thorny health issue, countless masks make appearances in stores. However, our company has launched an entirely different mask, a game changer that outshines our peers in the market. FIT Mask, a wearable device that combines the latest AI technology as well as great legacies from TCM (Traditional

Chinese Medicine).

You must be wondering why it's called FIT Mask. Literally, FIT means healthy. Our mask is the best fit for your health. More importantly, FIT perfectly summarizes our selling points.

Firstly, F stands for facial recognition. With this advanced technology and unique materials, our mask can adjust its shape to the unique geometry of your face, then memorize it, and recognize you when you put it on next time. In other words, this is a mask highly personalized to serve you, exclusively you.

Secondly, I stand for intelligence. Our mask is an intelligent health guardian. Equipped with a filter made of carbon fiber, it can make selective interception of harmful substances such as dust, germ and PM2.5. Moreover, it can keep track of your temperature, heartbeat and breath to produce a fitness scheme that suits you best, and can also sound early warnings if your health declines.

Last but not least, T stands for Traditional Chinese Medicine. In a FIT Mask, there is an ultra-thin layer that contains essence of TCM tonics and herbs that nurtures and improves your respiratory system. The more you wear it, the healthier you will get.

All in all, these three functions have transformed FIT Mask well beyond a mere shield against polluted air. It is a health guardian that not only protects you, but also cares about you. So, ladies and gentlemen, please, put it on. The moment you do it, you are embracing a safer and healthier world, with every breath fresher than ever!

Thank you very much, ladies and gentlemen.

（二）旅游类

Background

A study tour is generally defined as a trip taken by a group of people in order to carry out research. As for pre-college students, such tours often focus more on learning through experiencing. The key to a successful study tour for young students is finding a good balance between education and entertainment.

Student study tours are a fast-growing sector of China's tourism industry. On the one hand, more Chinese parents choose to send their children to domestic and foreign destinations during holidays to experience local cultures. On the other hand, students worldwide are coming to China to learn about its long history and diverse culture.

Task

Suppose you are the tour guide of a foreign study tour group coming to China. The group is comprised of 15 high school students from the UK. Design a one-day tour plan for the group and give them an oral introduction to the highlights of the day.

Requirements

- You can choose any destination in China.
- The tour plan must be practical and achievable in real-world situations.
- The introduction must be given in English.
- You have two minutes to deliver your introduction.
- You can and can only use static images（静态图片）as multi-media aids for your introduction.

【参考文章】

Ladies and gentlemen, I am your tour designer ×××from CITS and this is my partner ×××, your local guide.

Now, let me introduce our Chengdu Triple-I tour. Here, you will be fully immersed in profound history, internalize the local culture and be inspired by folk art.

Now comes the first I—history immersion. We will spend our morning in the world's oldest public high school, Chengdu Shishi Middle School[①], learning Chinese schooling history, studying traditional learning manners and admiring ancient Han architecture—Wanglouhanque.

Then, our exploration will continue as we move on to the second I—Culture internalization in Kuanzhai Alley.

Heading from east to west, we will be overwhelmed by the easy-going atmosphere. The living style of old Chengdu is so well preserved and presented in the lane. Looking around, people are enjoying the leisure. Listening around, friends are chatting. Lying down, we are having ear cleaning. With several minutes' ear massage and self-meditation, we can internalize the essence of Chengdu, comfort our anxious mind and get our body refreshed.

Finally, we will accomplish our tour with the third I—art inspiration in Jinli. There, we will taste authentic Chengdu Hot Pot while admiring legendary face changing in Sichuan Opera. With a flick of the wrist and a turn of the head, a child can become an evil monster, a fierce warrior or a pretty girl. You will have time to try on the costumes and have your face painted by the local professionals.

As the night falls, our Triple-I tour comes to an end. The spicy aroma of Sichuan culture is now for you to savor freely on your own. Wish you a nice trip and we sincerely hope to serve you again here in Chengdu.

二、2019 年

(一)商贸类

Background

With the development of modern technology, more and more smart household devices and appliances such as intelligent air conditioners and clean robots have come to our houses and make our life more convenient and comfortable. Next month an international Smart Home Exhibition will be held in London, which has drawn great interest of the local people. So far hundreds of local people have registered for free entries. They range in different ages from the young, the middle aged to the old people as well as in different professions.

Task

Suppose you are a marketing professional of a Chinese smart home company. Your company provides smart household devices and appliances which can "transform" houses and bring a smart life. Choose appropriate device(s) and appliance(s) and give a presentation to promote it or them to the possible buyers accordingly.

Requirements

- The products you choose must be practical and achievable in real-world situations.
- The presentation must be given in English.
- You have two minutes to deliver your presentation.
- You can and can only use static images(静态图片) as multi-media aids for your presentation.

现场互动(B 选手)Questions：

1. Can you name 3 smart features of your product?

2. What special preparation have you made for the UK Market?

---

① 成都石室中学 http://www.cdshishi.net/。

【参考文章】

Good afternoon, ladies and gentlemen, I am Sawn, sales manager of E-life company, joining me today is our R&D director Caroline, responsible for product upgrading and innovation.

When garbage sorting becomes new fashion, and resource recycling continues to be the hot spot issue of society, our company remains committed to our original aspiration, which is reducing waste and garbage.

Against this backdrop, our ECO fridge emerges as the time requires. With the help of the automatic scanning bar installed above the edge of our refrigerator's door, the expiry date of every item that comes into contact with the fridge will be spontaneously recorded, thus contributing to an eco-friendly life.

Are you still concerned about what to eat today or for the following days?

Thanks to the newest smart chip, our ECO fridge is fully capable of providing our customers and their loved ones with the ideal dietary choices according to the food available in the fridge. Besides, the AI recognition system will automatically match personal health data together with the customized recipes that contributes to physical fitness. Hence, it's time to say goodbye to obesity and diabetes but embrace a healthy and orderly life.

Tired of the hustle-and-bustle of the food market? Exhausted of rushing and squeezing into the supermarket during weekends? Once the fridge is out of supply, an automatic food supply request that is in line with our customers' eating habits will be sent from our fridge to Tmall Store. What's more, with a simple click on the smart food ordering pad, clients are granted with various food choices that they can flexibly choose whatever they want to eat.

ECO fridge is a fridge that incorporates the idea of ECO life, delivers this idea into customized service and has the function of an omnipotent housekeeper. ECO fridge, your best choice!

(二)旅游类

Background

A delegation of 5 members from New Zealand are attending a six-day long business meeting in Beijing. They have a very tight schedule and only have a day's break. They love Chinese culture such as the architecture, food, arts and also have great interest in Chinese history. So they want to take the chance and have a one-day tour in China. Since most of them have been to Beijing before, they prefer a tour outside Beijing. They also want to experience the high-speed train in China. The following is their simple memo in Beijing.

Date	Time	Things to do
DEC. 15	09:00—12:00 14:00—18:00	At the meeting the whole day
DEC. 16	09:00—12:00 14:00—18:00	At the meeting the whole day
DEC. 17	09:00—12:00 14:00—15:00	At the meeting the whole morning Free after 3 o'clock in the afternoon
DEC. 18		Free the whole day
DEC. 19	08:30—12:00 14:00—18:00	At the meeting the whole day (There is a very important seminar in the morning, and they will deliver a speech.)
DEC. 20	09:00—12:00 14:00—18:00	At the meeting the whole day

Task

Suppose you are their tour guide. Design a one-day tour plan for them and give an oral introduction to the highlights of the day.

Requirements

- You should first choose an appropriate destination for them in China.
- The tour plan must be practical and achievable in real-world situations.
- The introduction must be given in English.
- You have two minutes to deliver your introduction.
- You can and can only use static images(静态图片) as multi-media aids for your introduction.

现场互动(B选手)Questions：

1. Can you tell me 3 reasons for choosing this destination?
2. What measures will you take if we miss the train?

【参考文章】

Good morning ladies and gentlemen, what a pleasure to meet friends coming from afar! I am your tour guide Sherry from CITS and this is my partner Luna, your tour leader.

Unlike your hot springs for spa there, we have pure springs to drink here, in Jinan. These are natural wonders and kiwi sounds like wonders in Chinese, so today a special kiwi trip for kiwis, my dear New Zealanders.

To kindle your passion, we will take the fastest train, China Railway Fuxin, to approach Heihu Spring to experience locals' life: perch in a teahouse, sip tea made with sweet spring, and admire Shandong Allegro about spring history.

To involve ourselves in cultural landscape, we flow gently by boat in picturesque sceneries. On both sides, fine buildings like Liberate Pavilion and Spring City Square mirror ancient and modern in the light and you in turn become the sight in the eye.

Wander to Baotu Spring—"Number One Spring under the Heaven". Veiled with mist, the leaping splash is like boiling water, promising prosperity in business. More springs ahead, telling vigor and vitality.

To interact with spring culture, we arrive in Spring Studio. It applies MR and AR technology to fancy games for us to feel the past and future of spring culture, which may inspire a sparkling business idea.

Bathing in sunset glow, our kiwi trip ends with a bite of the spring banquet. Toast with a cup of spring tea: First sip, no more thirst; second sip, to be refreshed; third sip, friendship established. Wish you a joyful stay with us!

Let's go!

第二章 热身训练

训练,是选择过程。

在这个选择过程中,选手通过训练找到最适合参赛的自己,拥有最过硬的竞技储备,达到最佳竞技状态。

然而,大部分未经训练的选手都有轻微的舞台恐惧症,讲话没有表现力。那么,有目的地帮助选手打破束缚,提升表现力,提高语言流利度,树立表达自信,是训练课程的目标之一。不得不说,为备赛背诵词汇、记忆知识点、操练语言技巧,选手需要静下心,沉住气。备赛后期,比赛临近,学习量加大,压力随之而来,一些选手往往会在这时心生梦魇,对比赛望而却步。如果活动设计有趣味,团队之间有默契,有情感,有信任,不仅可以激发选手持续学习的动力,也会促使他们相互鼓励,相互扶持,继续前进。如何巧妙地"请君入瓮"和"有备无患"是指导老师在训练过程中一直在思考解决的事。

本章将从"鼓动人心""同舟共济""众说纷纭""珠行万里"四个方面讲一讲我们是如何引导兴趣,如何建设团队,如何打开学生视野,如何答好一道题,说好一个故事,如何学好语言与专业知识,掌握演讲技巧的。

第一节 鼓动人心

英语谚语"First impressions last."告诉我们,最初的印象往往最持久。因此,在培训技能大赛选手时,如何使用破冰游戏活跃气氛,调动学生的主观能动性,并为之后的团队建设夯实基础,是整个培训过程中非常重要的环节。编者认为,技能大赛训练课的破冰游戏应起到兴趣引入的作用,用和选手相关、来源于生活的有趣片段激发选手学习的欲望。其具体形式可包括创设情境、多媒体素材引入、由已知带动未知、以当前热点或争议话题引发探讨等。

本节内容精选了四个以破冰游戏为主的课例。

一、Icebreaker:Those dreams

以开放式问题引导选手思考,以思维导图(mind map)形式帮助选手理清思绪,培养逻辑性思维,并进行口语输出。

Teaching steps:

1. Lead in

The teacher shows a video / pictures of travelling and poses questions:

• Do you enjoy visiting different places?

• Did you go travelling recently? If yes, where did you go? If not, what holds you back?

Students may mention factors like lacking of money/time and then they are encouraged to think about another question:

• If you got enough money and time, where would you go for a vacation? Why?

2. Mind map: Where & Why

The teacher delivers paper to students and makes them write down the destination they prefer with reasons.

Students share their opinions in groups and write down the common points they've mentioned, such as local food and places of interest.

The teacher encourages students to compare common points with different groups and develop a mind map as follow.

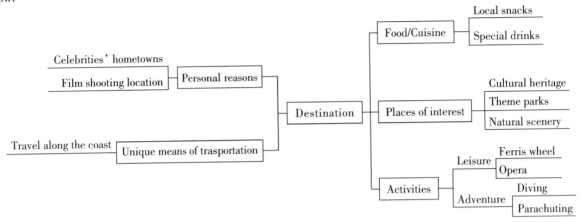

3. Develop your own mind map

Students search online for information about their destinations and complete a mind map of their own.

4. Presentation

Students take turns to introduce the chosen place and explain to the class why it's so attractive. While one student is delivering his speech, the others would complete the following form and mark 1-3 to show their interest in this place.

> The speaker mentions following aspects:
>
> □ Food
> □ Places of interest
> □ Activities
> □ Personal reasons
> □ Unique means of transportation
> □ Other aspects:_____
>
> I would mark _____ for this place according to his/her presentation.
>
> | 1 | 2 | 3 |
> |---|---|---|
> | not interested at all | would go there someday | can't wait to visit it |

Student who wins the highest score would get a prize from the teacher.

5. Extension

After finishing exercises above, the teacher needs to enhance students' understanding of the mind map, helping them to think logically and learn to structure their speeches.

The teacher poses other opening questions and students develop mind maps to organize their thoughts and then give presentations.

For example: If you found the Lamp of Aladdin, what do you want and why?

Mind map:

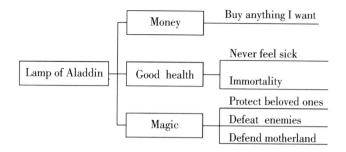

二、Icebreaker: A blind date

学生通过扮演"相亲"的角色来介绍该角色的性格特点,教师也可提供角色供学生选择。听众根据介绍和自己的兴趣投票,选出想要"相亲"的角色。建议按性别分别扮演介绍方和听众方,增加趣味。

Teaching steps:

1. The teacher teaches the rule of "How to describe a person / introduce a person" by inquiring students. The rule of NWWAAA is introduced here.

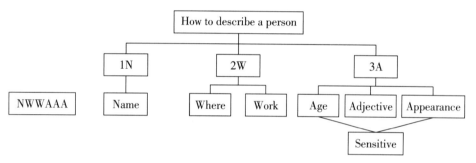

Teachers can start questions like "What do you want to know if you meet a new friend?"

2. Teach vocabulary of human's character, such as patient, loyal, devoted, not more than 10 words, using vocabulary games.

3. Introduce the "1 adj. +1 example" and have some practice.

The teacher tells students if they want to demonstrate the quality sb. has, they can tell audience an incident to reinforce the idea.

For example: I'd describe myself as a cheerful person. For instance, my colleagues said they felt more delightful when I was in the office. They have this feeling much stronger especially when I am assigned away from the office. One said she was used to my fun and humor every day.

4. Present yourself.

Try to sell yourself in the "human resources market" and try to get the most votes from your target audience. Students are going to practice the knowledge under the task of a blind date with the completion of task sheet and oral practice.

Who is the most charming gentleman/lady?(For teachers)
Step 1 Completing your sheet
Step 2 Making initial selection
Step 3 Marketing yourself in the market
Try to get votes as many as possible!

If you are the one!(For students)
1. 5 keywords to describe yourself
2. 1 typical incident that strongly shows your merits
Criteria for vote:
1. What do you want from your partner?
2. What does he/she have right now?
· Traditionally, a house and a car.
· Humorously, he has nothing but a cat and love.
Audience vote for their choice and give the reasons.

三、Icebreaker: Jigsaw puzzle poster and promoting

本节课旨在推动学生开展团队合作,提升分析能力。通过还原海报碎片、思考海报的特点、组成要素、宣传目的等,让学生在轻松愉快的氛围中围绕"海报"主题进行头脑风暴,构建思维框架。

Teaching steps:

1. The teacher mixes posters of 3 products and cuts the posters into several pieces. Then the teacher asks each pair of students to put pieces of the jigsaw puzzle together and find out the products on each poster.

2. The teacher leads students to think about and discuss the following questions:

- What makes a good poster?
- What are the essential parts of a poster?
- What's the purpose of using a poster?

3. The teacher invites students to share ideas and then gives them suggested answers.

- What makes a good poster?

Possible answer: readability, simplicity and originality (attractive title/slogan, eye-catching color)...

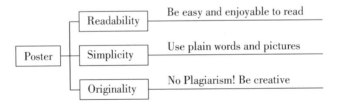

- What are the essential parts of a poster?

Possible answer: title/slogan, picture, character/product, numbers, other details...

- What's the purpose of using a poster?

Possible answer: present and promote products, boost sales...

4. Extension: Design a poster and promote yourself.

四、Icebreaker: Observe and talk—Will they date?

本节课的教学目的是使学生感受并初步建立训练团队的愉快氛围。学生通过观察一段非常有意义的视频,结合老师铺垫的一些知识做判断,建立礼仪知识,做到自信表达。

Teaching steps:

1. Warm-up

The teacher inquires questions "Do you expect anything to happen when you are on a journey to somewhere? Will you talk to some strangers?"

2. Raise the topic

The teacher introduces students to watch a video clip(12'30–15'30) *The Tourists* starred by Angelina Johnny and Jonny Depp. Students need to think about two questions after watching the scene.

① Who is more powerful?

② Will they date?

3. Offer two tools to help analyze the scene

The teacher invites students to watch the video again to dig out more details or evidence to reinforce their general impression about the episode. The two tools are:

①The extent of politeness

Action: Turn on the air-condition.

Teacher: What would you say if you want sb. to help you turn on the air-condition?

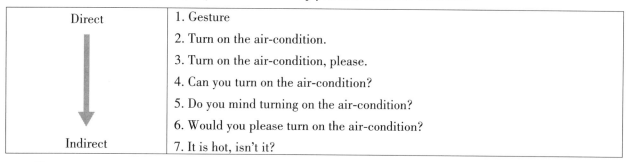

Direct ↓ Indirect	1. Gesture
	2. Turn on the air-condition.
	3. Turn on the air-condition, please.
	4. Can you turn on the air-condition?
	5. Do you mind turning on the air-condition?
	6. Would you please turn on the air-condition?
	7. It is hot, isn't it?

②Preferred/Dispreferred Action

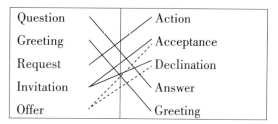

4. Watch the video the second time and think about the following questions with the tools

• Is the man interested in her?

• Who is more powerful?

• How do you know that?

Show me at least 3 pieces of evidence.

(Hint: Does she answer his questions? Who takes control of the topic? In what ways does she speak?)

5. Share the opinions

The teacher invites students to share the opinions. They can talk about what they find using the tools or something irrelevant but meaningful.

6. Improve the fluency

The teacher shows a sample answer to students.

【Sample answer】

In my opinion, the man Jonny Depp starred is interested in Angelina Julie. I can tell from his eye contact.

When she walked to him, he was reading a novel. Then when he realized the woman was sitting in front of him, he immediately dropped his book and stared at her.

Another point is that Angelina decided to sit there without asking for permission. She assumed that the man would allow her to sit there, while in the similar situation usually a stranger will ask "Is this seat taken?" for sure. Therefore, the woman shows she has more power.

第二节　同舟共济

通过第一节中充满趣味的游戏、小活动,课堂气氛活跃了起来,同学们增进了彼此间的了解,对学习英语也有了更大的兴趣,愿意展示自我能力,迎接更大的挑战。

此时教师可鼓励学生们自行组队完成任务,进行团队建设,从而培养合作意识,提高分析问题、解决问题的能力。在此过程中,教师要观察学生们的性格特点,如谁富有领导力,谁善于调和组内关系,谁思维活跃、创造性强,谁执行力强,能推动组内讨论,以便之后因材施教,并分配A、B角色,进行备赛组队。

一、Group project: SWOT analysis—pick the one

本节课旨在让学生了解SWOT分析的方法,并据此挑选出团队中最有领导力的成员,从而促使学生树立团队意识,也为今后合作训练夯实基础。

Teaching steps:

1. The teacher introduces today's task: learn SWOT analysis and form your team.

2. The teacher shows the most famous team: Tang Priest, Monkey King, Pigsy and Sandy.

3. The teacher asks students to guess the leader of this team and introduces concepts of SWOT.

Leader: Tang Priest

SWOT: S—strength; W—weakness; O—opportunity; T—threat

4. The teacher conducts a SWOT analysis of Tang Priest.

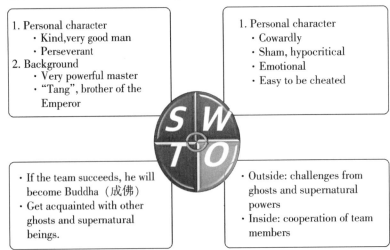

5. The teacher recaps the concepts of SWOT and asks students to finish a task.

• Draw the lot, find out your role—trainee? manager?

- Producer: Form a new group of 5 girls (Moonlight Girls) to debut (consider demands of the market and balance in the new group).

Criteria to consider
Vocal
Dance
Song writing
Appearance
Background
Previous experience

- Trainee: Try to be part of the group; fight for the Center; show your ability.
- Search the Internet about the idols you picked and finish your SWOT analysis.

二、Vocabulary games: Taboo

本节课旨在考查学生的词汇量和语言表达能力。学生以小组合作进行猜词竞赛，以提高默契度，增强团队荣誉感。根据规则，学生不能提及禁忌词，要快速思考从多个角度进行描述，展现应变和表达能力。

Teaching steps:

1. The teacher explains the meaning of "taboo" and divides students into groups of 4 or 5.

2. The teacher shows a target word with pictures and its "taboos" on PPT, and exemplifies how to guess the word without saying "taboos".

3. The teacher explains rules and tips.

Rules:

One student stands back to the whiteboard and others in the group describe target words in English without mentioning "taboos". The group which gets correct answers with the shortest time will win a small prize.

Tips:

- Each group has one chance to skip certain words.
- One "taboo" for 5 seconds added to the total time used.

4. Students work in groups to compete with others and win the final prize.

【拓展延伸】

指导老师可以用这个方式教授跟商贸、旅游相关的专业词汇，学生可以通过猜词和描述提升流利度和对单词的掌握程度。

三、Group Project: Design a role

本节课意图是让学生设计一款游戏。设计完成后，团队成员演绎作品，展示自己的亮点。学生通过团队合作，熟悉彼此，体验销售推广，积累经验。

1. Warm-up

The teacher asks students to talk about "What is your favorite e-game? Why? In this game, what role do you like best?"

2. Build up a team

Students are randomly divided into several groups of 4. After a team is organized, a team leader (boss), a notetaker and other roles in the "company" should be arranged through the discussion afterwards.

3. Analyse the similarities among popular games

Read the reading material *Living Video Games*[①], especially the underlined parts, and discuss the following questions with your group members:

- What are your favorite games?
- What elements do they have in common?

4. Talk about the game your company wants to design

Decide on the following information and then fill out the information in a report, which would be used to introduce your company (team).

- The names of your company and your company membes after class
- Your game name and game type
- Plot (the main idea of your game)
- Characters: Hero (Shero), the opponents, friends, or monsters
- Skills or weapons those characters need
- The reason why you design this game

5. Extension: Pick, Read and Act

Write down those scenes on cards. Other teams may randomly pick up the card. When the card is chosen, other teams need to act the scene written on the card. The corresponding card writer gives comments on the performance about whether they need to do some improvement, or the scene is exactly the writer describes.

第三节　众说纷纭

本项赛事紧跟时事热点,聚焦社会现象,旨在考查选手对新闻事件、热点问题的了解、看法,以及是否有能力给出合理的解决方案。回顾2018年—2019年的真题,不论是旅游类中的"乐学游"主题,还是商贸类试题中的"智能家居"和"寻找一样涉及环境保护的产品"都和近几年的时事热点有着紧密的联系。"乐学游"顺应了这几年青少年流行的游学主题,倡导在学习中娱乐,在游历中学习。参赛选手在设计旅行的过程中,寻找学习和游乐的平衡,在促进文化交流的同时也兼顾旅游带来的乐趣。而"智能家居"和"环境保护"这两个主题无一不响应了国家"智能驱动发展"和"绿水青山就是金山银山"的发展理念,让选手在参赛过程中能够切身感受和响应国家的号召。

为了能够充分迎合比赛需求,更好地帮助选手完成备赛过程,本书的编写团队精心挑选了和中职学生密切相关的时事热点,帮助选手做到有备无患。例如在商贸类中,我们挑选了"网红经济""新型奶茶""智能书店"等全新经营模式和产品以帮助选手了解科技驱动下的新型的销售模式和产业。

---

① Living Video Games 改编自 Paul Rooyackers 的 *101 More Drama Games for Children*。具体文件见附件。

通过上述概念和知识的渗透,选手能够在培训过程中加强辩证思考的能力、增进专业知识储备、提升英语语言应用能力,从而获得全方位的提升,取得较为理想的成绩。

一、The boom of bubble tea industry

教师通过网红奶茶,引入网红经济概念,让学生不仅能够积累相应的商贸知识,同时也了解到一杯小小的奶茶背后竟有着如此复杂的利益链条。

Teaching steps:

1. Lead in

As all kinds of industries are upgrading themselves to catch up with the changing market so as to take their hold in the market, bubble tea industry is no exception. Grabbing a cup of bubble tea and having a pleasant talk with your best friends at a cozy shop is a wonderful choice when it comes to spending our days off.

Questions:

1. Which brand of bubble tea is your favorite?

2. How did bubble tea go viral? Is it because of its exceptional taste, unique package or outstanding quality?

3. What is the story behind the successful marketing?

Think about the elements that lead these brands to success.

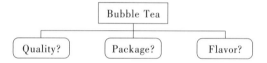

Possible answer: Celebrity plus economy.

2. The teacher continues the inquiry: What is Internet celebrity economy?

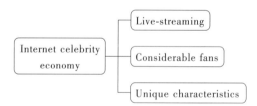

3. The teacher asks students to establish their own bubble tea brand by drawing a mind map.

Students can take the following elements for reference when drawing the mind map.

- Name of drinks—Rule: catchy and rhythmic.
- Decoration style, flavor, health, price, location and others.

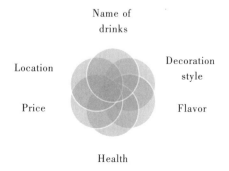

4. Open questions:

①Is it worthwhile to wait for hours to get their bubble tea solely for taking pictures and sharing them on moments?

②What will the future market be for bubble tea?

e.g. Take <u>Starbucks</u> as an example which went global and achieved unprecedented success.

二、Smart bookstores

本节课以电商时代为背景,以实体书店为切入点,让学生不仅能够亲历实体书店为了适应新时代、新背景转型升级的过程,同时收获新型智能书店运营模式、创新举措等相应知识,为商贸知识后期的学习打下坚实基础。

Background information

In the age of smart life, we are too often engulfed by the hustle and bustle of fast-paced life. Luckily, there are places where we can temporarily leave our desire, anxiety behind. This is the charm of urban bookstores. Having gone through the tough years against the challenges brought by online bookstores, brick and mortar bookstores have successfully transformed themselves to cater for the changing need of consumers, and smart bookstores with puppies, cats and ingenious beverages are the best answer.

1. Warm up

The teacher asks questions to simulate students' thinking.

① Why brick and mortar shops no longer enjoy their heyday?

② Are there any ways or methods that you can help them to regain popularity?

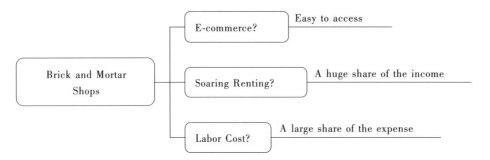

Possible answer:

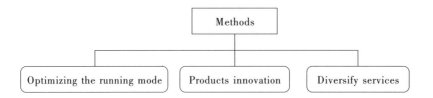

2. Video lead-in

Students watch a video demonstrating the changes that a bookstore had undertaken against the wave of e-commerce so as to keep itself within the fierce competition. Students are required to make a comparison between the bookstore in the video and the traditional bookstores in our daily life. Taking notes is welcomed while watching.

Key points need to be caught from the video:

• Running mode

- Advantages
- What will happen if the shop stops making innovation?
- How to instill the idea of innovation/smart into brick and mortar shops?

Keys:

Smart operating mode	Traditional business model
Books+coffee+culture innovation Stationery Cozy space Lighting Color of the furniture	Selling books and videos

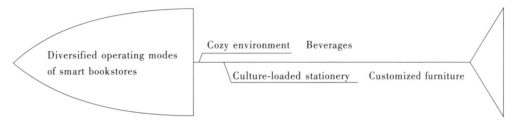

3. The teacher raises further questions to engage students in thinking.

① How to instill the idea of smart into bookstores? (Open question)

Possible answers:

- Postcards mailed to you in the near future.
- Bookmarks elegantly made with ingenious design.
- Providing local cuisines whenever you step into the shop.

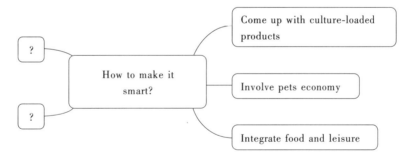

② Stop making innovation, then what will happen?

Possible answers:

- Unable to maintain their market status.
- Lose market share and hard to make ends meet.

4. Group work

Design your ideal smart bookstore and present it to your peers.

三、Keep in pace: The Corona Virus

本节课以新冠肺炎疫情为背景,通过科普病毒相关知识,让学生养成良好的卫生习惯,加强疫情防控意识,发扬生命至上、举国同心、舍生忘死、尊重科学、命运与共的新时代抗疫精神。

Teaching steps:

1. Greeting and lead-in

The teacher asks students to talk about their winter holiday and the reason about the extension of this holiday.

2. The teacher introduces the concept of Corona Virus and its official name COVID-19.

3. The teacher highlights the vocabulary related to the topic.

4. The teacher asks students to watch a video[①] and take notes about the main idea and major facts.

5. The teacher plays the video again and asks students to answer following questions:

- What's the appearance of corona viruses?

- Where did the virus come from?

- How is it transmitted?

- What are the symptoms?

- How can we tell whether someone is infected?

- How to stop the transmission of the virus?

6. The teacher shares some pictures on the topic of COVID-19 which are adapted from world - famous paintings.

7. The teacher invites students to share measures taken for fighting against Corona Virus. (30" –1' brief presentation)

四、Keep in pace: Movers and Shakers in China

随着生活品质的提升和逐渐加速的城市化,越来越多的人开始涌入城市,而相应的链条式服务也应运而生。学生能够从不同品质的搬家服务一窥产品结构、任务分工、定价依据等一系列涉及商贸知识的专业概念,从而在准备自己的商品时能做好一系列的事先预备工作。

1. Lead in

As China is becoming increasingly more urbanized, more people and businesses start to make their moves around cities. In an environment where time comes at premium, a market has opened up to include moving services. While EZ mover company[②] is more expensive than most traditional moving companies in China, its customers don't have to lift a finger other than type in their relevant information on their WeChat account. The

---

① https://mp.weixin.qq.com/s/Bqg67RV9F9N3z-orxVIZJA。

② https://www.e-zmovers.com/about-us。

price is determined by the number of movers, distance, volume of the freight, etc.

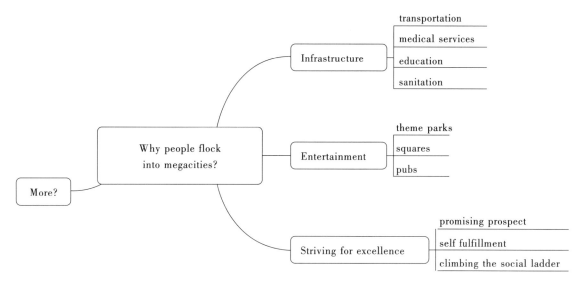

The teacher asks "Who needs the moving service the most when living in a metropolitan? How much do you think it will cost if you order a moving service online?"

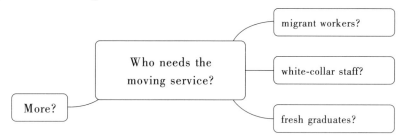

2. Exercise

Based on your preclass research about moving service, please answer the following questions.

Questions:

①What's the features/highlights of EZ mover company?

②What's the feature of "蓝犀牛"① company?

Possible answers:

①Mirror Japanese business model

    High quality one-stop service

    White collars having no time to deal with moving

    High-end market

②Match up user and potential moving services

    Pricing system is very clear and transparent.

    It is not likely to run into disagreements with customers.

3. Discussion

What's the advantages and drawbacks of EZ mover company?

---

① http://lanxiniu.com/。

Possible answers:

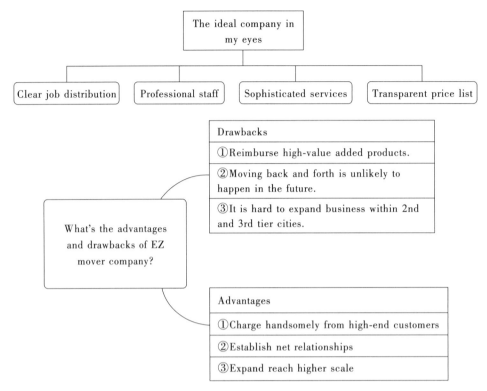

4. Design your ideal company

Students are suggested to take the following elements into their presentation.

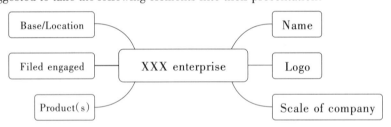

第四节　珠行万里

通过第一章的内容,相信指导老师对于选手的语言综合实力有了一定的评判标准。本书的编者团队一致认为,在整个大赛环节中,虽然B选手展现的时间较A短,但却更考验选手的功夫。训练队的集结和整个训练计划的安排其实就是围绕提高选手的语言综合实力和临场应变能力而展开的。在训练过程中,指导老师要找到适合完成B选手应答环节的种子选手。

根据历届选手的现场的真实回答,经过适当转码编写,我们选出了6份回答。商贸组、旅游组各三份,每组按欠佳、适中、优秀编排,并根据我们推理的得分点,在问题最后给出答案解析,供读者参考。

现场互动问答通常有两道问题,第一道题与A选手所展示的产品内容相关,第二道题通常是相关专业的知识储备问题。第二道题较第一道题难度更大,灵活性更高。这道题更容易区分出选手的语言水平高低和职场知识多少,从而在分数上拉开各组间的差距。在平时训练时,带队老师也应在第二道题上花下精力,做足功夫。

一、商贸类

Question: What special preparation have you made for the UK Market?(评委针对 Eco fridge 产品演讲后的提问,即 2019 年商贸组主题产品营销。)

Inadequate answer:

May I beg your pardon, well (pause), it is a good question. For the UK Market, we have made a lot of preparations, so I think our product is the best one (pause). It has three outstanding features and will be liked by the UK customers (pause)... Second, it is very cheap. Hmm, it is also very good, for example, it can tell people a lot of things. And lastly, children will love it. They ask their parents to buy it, so it will be popular. (time is up)

Moderate answer:

Well, because Britain is now entering into an aging era, which means there is a large need in the health-care field for aging people, so our product will gradually take over the market share. To begin with, it can inform old people about the right time to take medicine to let them become healthier. (pause) Second, our smart machine will also talk with them when they are bored, so they won't feel lonely. And most importantly, our product is very smart, it can monitor the health condition of the old, so their sons or daughters can focus on their work instead of looking after them. So all these things are very useful.

Satisfactory answer:

Thank you for your question. As we're going to take hold of the UK Market, we've made comprehensive R&D plan together with customer background surveys before we launch our product. First, our smart scanning bar can effectively resolve food-waste phenomenon in the UK, which can contribute greatly to environment protection. Second, customized recipes provided by our product will help eradicate chronic diseases, like obesity, high-blood pressure, etc., which have troubled British people for more than centuries. Lastly, senior citizens are freed from the hustle and bustle of the food market with all the food being ordered and delivered from the online market, thus they are not likely to tumble on the way to the market or run into an argument when grabbing the last bundle of "today's special". All the edges mentioned above will surely make our product the most sought-after in the UK Market.

问题"对进军英国市场有何特殊准备"旨在考查选手在职业场景中的英语应用能力,体现了职业模块"能用英语初步处理简单的常规业务"的教学内容与要求。此类问题对选手的要求较高。第一,选手要对本组产品的特点了如指掌;第二,选手要对市场需求有深入了解,知道消费者的偏好;第三,选手要将产品特点和市场需求进行一一对应地讲解,做到有理有据。

以本题为例,选手应首先明确本组产品的特点,如智能扫描保质期、个性化菜单、网上订购食品等;其次,选手应对英国市场进行分析,归纳市场特点,如经济较发达、社会水平高、人口老龄化严重等;最后,选手应针对英国市场特点对产品进行解读,展示该产品如何符合当地的市场需求以及针对消费者偏好做了哪些特殊准备。

在此框架下,三个层次的答案水平差异显著。欠佳的答案回答不充分,造成这一问题的原因可能为:1. 选手听的能力较弱,无法获取主要信息,对个别单词的发音,如 preparation 不熟悉,造成理解障碍。因此,在回答问题时,以"May I beg your pardon..."开头,想要再听一遍题目,重新理解题意,浪费了答题时间。

2. 在限定时间内,因思维水平未达到相关要求,无法有效组织语言,形成有意义的回答。例如,在文中出现的"it can tell people a lot of things"中,代词 it 和 things 所指的概念模糊不清。3. 受语言能力所限,出现较多停顿、忘词以及重复信息,无法顺畅准确表意。在该回答中,一共出现三次停顿,其中一次停顿时间较长,并直接跳到了第二个要点。4. 答题时间分配不合理。

　　一般答案基本达到相关要求。1. 信息接收效率较高,能正确理解问题意图。选手在回答中点明了"...Britain is now entering into an aging era...",对老年人养护产品需求高,从而推导出自身的产品将逐渐占领英国市场这一论点。2. 回答条理较为清晰,且能够较为流畅地表达要点。To begin with, second, most importantly 三个连接词将要点进行有效连接。但遗憾的是:1. 思考的时间造成的停顿导致时间不够,答案的信息量不足。2. 在罗列自身产品特点时,句式较为单一,基本都是因果关系的句子。用词不够多样化,so 高频出现。

　　优秀的答案在适中答案的基础上更加优化。1. 信息接收效率高,正确理解问题意图并在回答中加以拓展和深化。例如,回答中提到了英国的食品浪费现象(food-waste phenomenon)与环保思潮(environment protection),私人订制菜谱(customized recipes)与慢性病频发(chronic diseases),老龄化社会(senior citizens)与网上商城(online market),每个要点中的两个概念看似矛盾,但选手皆能自圆其说,可见构思精巧。2. 回答结构清晰,逻辑严密。整个回答从主旨句点明论点开始,用产品的三个特性对应英国市场的三大特点,再用总结句强调论点、收束全文,结构非常完整。3. 用词精准地道,避免重复,例如 take hold of, comprehensive R&D plan, launch our product, hustle and bustle 等。语句类型也非常多样化,用到了定语从句、状语从句、被动语态、因果关系连词(as, thus)等,可见选手功力之深。4. 赛场礼仪和答题习惯好。在接到提问之后,先感谢评委的问题,再娓娓道来,从容应对,在印象分上就先胜了一局。整篇回答在以上优点的基础上,还保持了语意连贯、表达流畅的特点,行云流水,一气呵成。

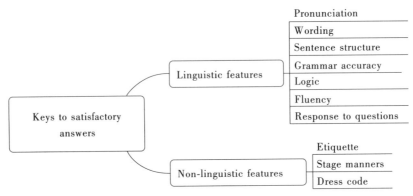

二、旅游类

Question: What measures will you take if we miss the train?(2019年旅游组评委所提第2问。)

Inadequate answer:

Uh, sorry, could you please repeat the question? ... Hmm, I think we can do something to ... to help our guests. If we miss the train, we can ... we can explain to them why we miss the train so that they won't be too angry after knowing the reason. And ... we can ... maybe find some other trains' tickets, or ... let them do something else if we miss the train ... can't go to Jinan...

Moderate answer:

Thank you. If we miss the train... if it really happens... I think we'll take some actions. For example, we can check on the app to see if there're available tickets for the next train to Jinan, book tickets immediately and tell our guests to catch the next train. Besides, we'll let our guests know that we're very sorry about the inconvenience and are trying our best to solve the problem. That's all, thank you.

Satisfactory answer:

Well, thank you for your question. As experienced tour guides, we always make full preparations in advance and get a plan B. First, we'll apologize sincerely and comfort our guests, and let them know such an incident won't affect our trip seriously. Second, we'll book alternative tickets and take the next train to Jinan, thus reducing the negative effect to a minimum. Third, if it's our fault, we'll make up for it, e.g. offer some gifts or vouchers. However, as I mentioned before, we're professional and considerate, so we'll remind ourselves and guests of the schedule beforehand, and never let such incidents happen.

该题角度刁钻,所以我们在训练和冲刺阶段不仅要在意导游的品质、产品的亮点、旅游中介的营销手段和售后服务,还要在意这个服务性行业的职业特色:即使做了万全准备,也会有意外。此题考查的就是在突发状况下,从业人员的应急处理和思辨能力。

从旅游专业角度上看,我们要思考:

1."为什么"会错过火车。是先前准备不足,自己或游客迟到,有不可抗力,如天气变化、交通安全检查等,还是当地、经过地发生了问题? 选手在赛前应对此类突发状况做到心中有数,并在答题时择其一二,阐述应对策略。

2."怎么办"。既然已经错过时间了,我该提供怎样的解决办法,怎样安抚游客的心情? 解决办法有哪些? 首先,选手要决定还去不去旅游地,去的话能否搭下一班车,是否需要切换交通工具;不去的话,又有什么解决方案,是在酒店里休息,还是游览当地景点? 无论去不去目的地,选手都应说明因误车而损失的时间对原计划行程是否造成影响,让游客(评委)做到心中有数。上述解决措施都是对当天的行程安排做的弥补,选手挑选哪一种都可以,但要说得清晰、简洁、有逻辑性。

3."什么态度"。作为旅游从业者,出现这么大的变故,什么样的态度可以获得理解,也可以被接受? 答案应是谦虚、诚恳的态度。在这个问题上,导游应先道歉,尔后解释原因并提供补救措施,最后对意外做相应补偿。如果选手能考虑到这几点,那么在职业和思维上的得分就几近满分。

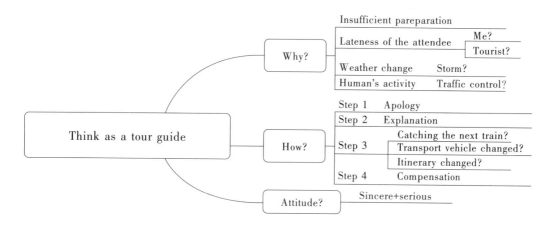

我们再从3份回答的语言内容方面做分析。首先是获取信息的能力。很明显,第一位选手没有听清楚并请求评委重复问题(Uh, sorry, could you please repeat the question?)。这在比赛现场很致命,因为它不仅浪费时间,拉低了印象分,更体现出选手对导游应对突发状况的准备不足。第二名选手应变能力较强,以"If we miss the train... if it really happens..."重复问题来为自己赢得思考时间,方便作答。第三名选手则显然胸有成竹,有备而来。

其次是组建回答架构,展现逻辑性思维的能力。第一名选手基本是想到什么说什么,回答缺少层次感。第二名选手能理清思绪,运用for example, besides等词比较流畅地连接语句;在回答内容上比第一位选手更贴近现实,比如提到check on the app。第三位选手用了first, second这样层层递进的词汇串联回答——表明态度——提供解决方案——做出补偿,逻辑非常清晰,表现出他是真的在设身处地思考并解决这个问题。每位选手并不一定非要使用递进词,但也应注意理清思路,组织语言,便于评委抓取得分点。

再次是语言输出能力,其中涵盖了词汇、句型、流利度、时间掌控等多个方面。第一名选手有比较多的停顿,不够自信流利;在词汇选择上过于简单,句式变化也不多,语言水平可见一斑。第二位选手的词汇量和表达水平相较第一位选手更彰显功力,如使用immediately, take some actions等,语言也更为流利,少有磕绊。第三名选手明显水平更高,用了in advance, experienced, book alternative tickets, reducing negative effect等,在表示歉意时不是简单地说sorry,而是用apologize sincerely。该生的回答,在词汇选择、句式搭配和流利度上都做到了极致。

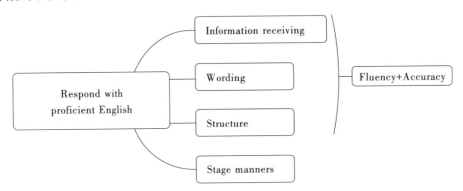

最后是仪态、发音等整体形象。选手应做到落落大方,自信从容,在台上不摇头晃脑,不做挠头等小动作;单词发音正确,语调自然;对评委保持礼貌尊敬,面带微笑。

第三章 专业知识及思维训练

技能大赛的A、B两位选手不仅要展示自己的英语风采、舞台表现能力,同时也要在语言表现上,体现出自己深厚的专业功底,尤其是对专业知识的理解掌握。那么在前期培训上,我们不仅使用如上的语言活动丰富我们的训练课堂,调动我们学生的学习兴趣,同时,专业知识的铺垫也尤为重要。本章节将根据两个赛项的特点,分别讨论编委会一致认为在技能大赛中必须掌握的相关知识。

第一节 专业知识

一、征战商场——商贸知识

(一)What Is Marketing?

Marketing refers to activities a company undertakes to promote the buying or selling of a product or service. Marketing includes advertising, selling, and delivering products to consumers or other businesses. Some marketing is done by affiliates on behalf of a company.

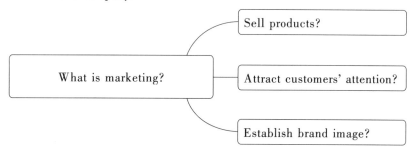

Key points:

• Marketing refers to all activities a company does to promote and sell products or services to consumers.

• Marketing makes use of the "marketing mix", also known as the four Ps[1] and four Cs[2]—product, price, place and promotion and customer, cost, communication and convenience.

• At its core, marketing seeks to take a product or service, identify its ideal customers, and draw customers' attention to the product or service.

---

① 菲利普.科特勒:《市场营销:原理与实践》,北京:中国人民大学出版社,2015年,第54—56页。

② https://www.toolshero.com/marketing/4c-marketing-model/。

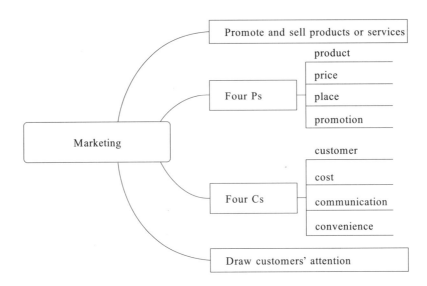

（二）Applying SWOT strategy into marketing

What is SWOT? SWOT analysis (or SWOT matrix, Weihrich, 1982) is a strategic planning technique used to help an organization identify strengths, weaknesses, opportunities and threats related to business competition or project planning.

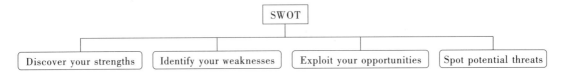

Application

In order to conduct a relatively comprehensive analysis of the situation an organisation faces in the market, enterprises of all sizes and marketers of different levels will resort to the help of SWOT strategy as it can provide a reasonable and straightforward research of its internal value and external identification.

As Heinz Weihrich(1982) suggested, firstly we need to define our business area. Then think about opportunities, like political, economic, social and technological developments, and threats, risks or dangers arise from the environmental factors. Depict future scenario and identify internal strengths, like competitive advantages and weaknesses such as what should be improved or eliminated.

With identified SWOT, strategies and tactics should be planned and developed afterwards.

Below are two SWOT examples.

Example 1: Analysis of a market position of a small management consultancy with specialism in HRM short form for human resource management.

Strengths	Weaknesses	Opportunities	Threats
Reputation in the marketplace	Shortage of consultants at operating level	Well established position with a well-defined market niche	Large consultancies operating at a minor level
Expertise at partner level in HRM consultancy	Unable to deal with multi-disciplinary assignments because of the size or lack of ability	Identified market for consultancy in areas other than HRM	Other small consultancies looking to invade the marketplace

Example 2: Analysis of Xiaomi Corporation

Strengths	Weaknesses	Opportunities	Threats
Self-innovated user system	Off-paint problem	Less fierce market as Samsung and Apple company gradually losing their share in China	More and more smart phone developers are joining the battle field of mobile phones
Less promotion cost (cutting back the fee of inviting spokespeople)	Temporary crashing issue	Increasing need for smart mobile phones	Obstacles in developing certain application because of the limitation of Android system

（三）Scenarios relating to marketing

1. Online marketing

Here we adopt two prime examples to show the full picture of online marketing in which well-known social-media influencers in China, sell products of all kinds during their live-streaming period and create unprecedented records in terms of online sale. On top of live-steaming, we also take Apple company's success into consideration, which shaped its unique marketing method and led to an unparalleled success in history.

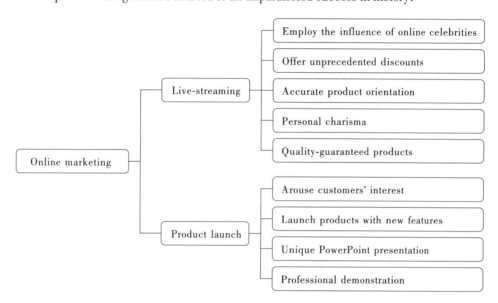

Strategies behind online marketing triumph—live-streaming

i. Adopt exaggerated expressions to boost consumption desire

ii. Shorten the distance by using affectionate addressing (using emotional words to lead the audience)

iii. List credible data to dispel customers' concern

iv. Highlight words such as "coupon" and "discount" so as to attract more customers

v. Cite self-experience of certain products to make it more convincing

vi. Involve intimate interaction in live-streaming period

Apple company's tactics in marketing

i. Interpret products with professional terms

ii. Emphasize the cost-effectiveness of its product

iii. Use technological elements to enhance customers' perception of its new products

iv. Create scenarios for the use of its products so as to arouse customers' purchasing desire

2. Off-line marketing

Experience stores together with road shows are typical examples when referring to off-line marketing. Customers are more likely to be tempted when having close interaction with products as they set their foot into the experience stores and road shows somehow will arouse their buying desire to some extent because of the manifestation of its on-site show.

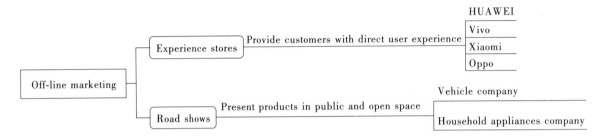

Features of HUAWEI experience stores

i. On-site interpretation of different products to meet the needs of various customers.

ii. Professional advice to customers' doubts and worries.

iii. Timely help when problems arise.

iv. Real-interaction experience by providing the actual products.

v. Proper accessories relating to other products so as to generate more profits.

Characteristics of road shows

i. Create an atmosphere and environment that attracts more potential customers.

ii. Provide customers with real-life experience.

iii. Hold interactive activities to boost brand image.

iv. Offer professional advice when people start to consult.

v. Establish customer network by talking and sharing contact information.

3. In-sale service

In-sale service is the service provided by salespeople during the sales process and based on deep understanding of customers' demands.

（四）What is e-commerce?

E-commerce or electronic commerce refers to business transactions conducted through the use of electronic appliances (such as ATM, fax, smartphone, tablet and computer) without the exchange of paper documents.

E-commerce can be characterized as the following 4 categories:

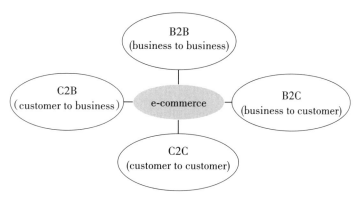

The advantages and disadvantages of e-commerce are listed as follows:

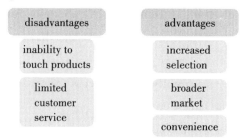

（五）What is customer relationship management?

Customer relationship management refers to maintaining relationship with existing and potential customers. Customers' requirements need to be understood, and their needs and expectations need to be fulfilled. A typical customer relationship cycle follows:

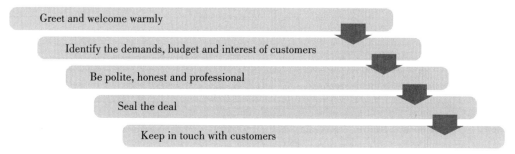

Step 1: Greet and welcome warmly

Warm greetings and welcome can be regarded as the beginning of customer relationship, the assurance of reliable recommendation and the prime element of a good impression.

Step 2: Identify the demands, budget and interest of customers

Thorough research and deep understanding of customers' demands, budget and interest usually lead to accurate position of products and suitable recommendation for customers.

Step 3: Be polite, honest and professional

Providing service with politeness, honesty and profession is a key to harmonious customer relationship.

Step 4: Seal the deal

It is important to seal the deal complying with the TPO principle—that is to say—consider the Time, Place and Occasion during business negotiation and make the deal happen.

Step 5: Keep in touch with customers

Don't forget your customers after the deal. Remember existing customers always bring potential customers in the near future.

Related scenarios

Here we adopt two prime examples to show the full picture of e-commerce in the form of promotion and discount on Double 11 in Taobao and June 18th in JD. The success of these two shopping carnivals thoroughly influenced the shopping behavior of customers and created unprecedented records every year in terms of its turnover. When it comes to customer relationship management, we take Apple Store as an example, which follows the customer relationship cycle to conclude a business transaction.

E-commerce: promotion and discount on Double 11 in Taobao & June 18th in JD

With the development of e-commerce, regular promotion and discount on festivals already make online e-commerce platforms gain large profits. Among all the festivals, Double 11 in Taobao and June 18th in JD are most lucrative in terms of income. Apparently, their success shares some similarities.

- Only set one date in a year for the largest promotion.
- Third-party payment, like Alipay and WeChat, is accepted.

However, the differences between these two platforms are rather obvious.

	Taobao	JD
Category	C2C	B2C
Payment	Payment before delivery	Payment before or on delivery
Logistics	Third-party logistics combined	Self-built logistics system
Storage	No	Several warehouses
Promotion mode	Coupon, membership discount, discount varies from individual merchants	Coupon, membership discount, discount in proprietary commodities
Revenue through promotion	The platform works on commission and gains extra from merchants who are bidding for promotion	Mostly from proprietary commodities (very few cost on distribution and promotion)
Customer service	Service coordinators need to negotiate with individual merchant to settle the problem; Sometimes time-consuming and unpleasant solution	Customer service commissioner directly responds to customers' problems; Timely feedback, usually with satisfactory solution

Customer relationship management: Genius Bar in Apple Store

Let's take a look at the brand Apple again.

Genius Bar in Apple Store provides with both online and off-line customer service and support. Customers can get professional advice through channels like instant messages, phone calls and emails, usually with satisfactory solutions to software and service problems. For hardware problems, customers can make a Genius Bar appointment and get help face to face from an expert in the Apple Store. All the recount and request of customers will be put on record for further reference.

（六）After-sales service

1. What is after-sales service?

After-sales service refers to all the things you do for the care and feeding of your valued customers after they buy your product. This type of customer aftercare is vital for any business, but especially for small businesses where every client counts.

Why after-sales services matter?

The more you care your customers, the more they're likely to support you right back with their loyalty and enthusiasm. They'll become the brand ambassadors, reviewers, and trusted voices who'll give you great reviews, sing your praises on social media, and give you honest feedback on new products and features.

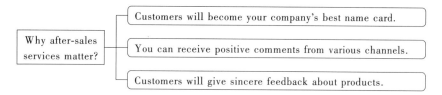

2. An introduction to 6 most common types of after-sales service

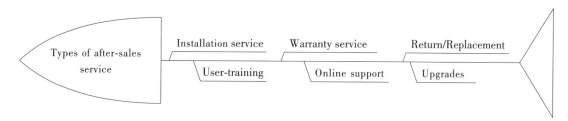

①installation service

The installation service initiates once the transaction is done. Depending on the nature of the product, the installation procedure may vary. Some installations can be user-friendly, like mobile phones and toys which don't require sophisticated process whereas some require professional expertise, such as washing machines, air conditioners, etc.

②User-training

Training of the end user is an indispensable part of after-sales service that applies to various fields, especially to professions requiring accurate performances. Taking the doctor as an example, in the process of a surgical operation, it is very essential that the doctor has to get trained before using the machine in case that there are potential risks. Successful companies like Apple and HUAWEI all provide their customers with detailed user-training service after the transaction so as to guarantee the best user experience.

③Warranty service

Warranty service is perhaps the most common type of after-sales service provided by almost every company for almost every product. It includes repairing and replacement of selected or the whole product in a selected period of time. For example, Apple Company provides "Apple care" that guarantees the maintenance of its product effective from the date you buy their product and customers are given the option to extend their warranty period by whether renew their "Apple care" service before the end of the official warranty.

④Online support

Distant support can be of great value to those overseas and remote users who are not likely to conduct a present inquiry which for the most of the time can be troublesome and time-consuming. With detailed and systematic online support, customers can not only solve technical problems when using their products, but also become more literate in terms of using their product. Online support is very effective for software services and laptop support as staff responsible for customer service can share the screen and resolve the problem immediately in most of the cases.

⑤Return/Replacement

Every company has its own terms and conditions when it comes to refund whether it is for a selected part or the whole piece. For most of the companies, they provide free replacement service of a product effective from the date when customer buys the product. However, this is in line with certain terms and conditions. In some cases, replacement may be of the entire device, or in other cases, replacement may be only of the defective part.

⑥Upgrades

This kind of service usually applies to software and electronics that need to optimize itself to better serve customers. Always catching up with the newest trend and a company is likely to be ruled out when stopping making innovations are the natural rules in the field of science and technology.

3. Five practices for establishing strong customers relationships

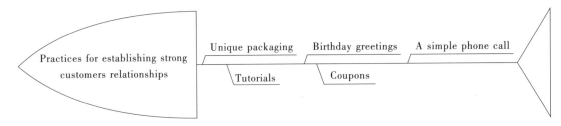

①Unique packaging

Ingenious design with distinctive style is the best name card for promoting one's product, as customers will naturally get a sense of pride of holding the bag and carrying it around the area they live, which is the best endorsement for the product. Eye-catching packaging can also be a powerful selling point since it can not only grab the attention of potential customers, but also partly reflect its company's dedication into every detail of its product not to mention the quality.

②Coupons

Offering coupons to previous customers is an effective way to expand business and increase sales. A good user experience will likely to appeal to the customers again to make the same purchase at the same store. Moreover, they may introduce the products to their families, friends and providing them with the coupons will double the chance to conduct the deal.

③A simple phone call

A sincere follow-up call after the first week use of the product plus polite greetings and professional guidance will strengthen the customer relationship and contribute to the establishment of company's image. You're expected to note down customers' feedback and answer possible questions. Easy the task may seem, but hard to perform in real-life scenario. Remember: try not to promote other products and listen attentively in the conversation. If they don't answer the phone, don't sweat it; leave them a simple message of thanks for their business and let them know you're available to answer questions.

④Tutorials

A tutorial or mini-lecture to some extent can be of great help when products are malfunctioning or the operating procedure is hard to implement. Customers will receive useful instructions informing them about the features of their products and tricks to employ their products to the full extent, thus you're once again helping your company to build a group of loyal users.

⑤Birthday greetings

Don't underestimate the power of a timely "Happy Birthday!" Either an email or a short message can leave a good impression to your customers. It can recall your customers' fading memory about their purchase at your company and provide them with certain benefits, such as little presents or coupons will only make them the happiest guy in their birthday.

4. After sales

①Related scenarios: Handling customers' complaints

Handling customers' complaints is important in after-sales process. The purpose of it is to ensure satisfaction of customers and steady improvement of a company. Dealing with customers' complaints usually covers the following steps:

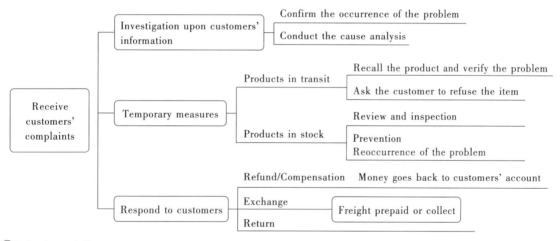

②Telephone follow-up

It is essential to conduct telephone follow-up after responding to customers' complaints. Through telephone follow-up, instant feedback of customers' attitude can be recorded, further problems can be spotted, potential problems can be prevented. The process of a successful telephone follow-up can be seen as:

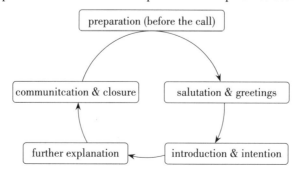

（七）Vocabulary list for this module

marketing 市场营销	membership discount 会员折扣
marketing mix 市场营销组合	proprietary commodities 自营商品
SWOT analysis 企业战略分析法（内部优势、劣势,外部机会、威胁）	commission 佣金
	service coordinator 客服调解员
comprehensive 综合性的	time-consuming 费时的
social-media influencer 网络红人	after-sales service 售后服务
live-streaming（流媒体）直播	refund 退款
product launch 产品发布会	installation 初始化安装
cost-effectiveness 成本效益	warranty 保修期
experience store 体验店	replacement 换货
road show 路演;巡回演出宣传	upgrade 升级换代
e-commerce 电子商务	complaint 投诉
payment 支付方式	compensation 赔偿
logistics 物流	freight prepaid 运费预付
storage 仓储	telephone follow-up 电话回访
warehouse 货仓	

二、纵旅天下

（一）Part 1　Planning

In most cases, planning proceeds travelling. As a travel agency, we offer not only tours with established schedules and routes but also customized itineraries for customers. Here, with the consideration of the competition, we focus more on the latter type.

When our customers knock our door to seek tourism service, we are obliged to offer the most professional services to cater for them. In addition, we should obey some rules and consider several following issues when we design a tourism product.

We always carry out the following strategy to design a tour. The following elements are always taken into account and considered back and forth when we attempt to offer the best, impressive, suitable and sensible tour services to cutomers.

1. The strategy of planning a tour

a. Decide where to visit—the destination and places of interest.

b. Do relevant research (eg. tickets, fare, history, famous people, activities in the season, exhibitions and/or something worth seeing).

c. Design a(n) route/itinerary.

d. What we need to prepare in our package.

e. Time, fee, experience and other tour guides or tourists' feedback are taken into consideration. We spent least time and money to enjoy ourselves in most places.

f. Adjust and finalize the itinerary.

2. Principles for designing a tourism product/route

Tour guides are expected to create wonderful travel memories for guests and deal with emergencies during the trip, not simply counting heads or distributing tickets. An experienced tour guide will always bear guests' needs in mind, provide high-quality service and solve problems in a professional manner.

The rules in the planning phase can be concluded as "impressive, cost-effective, wonderful and safe".

"Impressive" means when the journey is done, tourists still remember the theme or some exquisite parts of the trip, either activities or meals. We can interpret "impressive" into another understanding. When our contestants complete their speech, something must be left in judges' mind.

"Cost-effective" means each coin we spend makes its value. Tourists enjoy the journey. No penny is wasted.

"Wonderful" means the wonderful journey brings wonderful memories. The routes should be interesting and comforting.

"Safe" would be not necessary to explain too much. No one expects danger.

3. How to finalize on a destination?

①Customers' features and their needs

First, we should consider our customers' features and needs (see in the following section), like the nationality, hobby, time, occupation, age and finance. Customers' tastes and needs always weigh much. Last but not least, what message we try to deliver to our customers and how we can impress them are critical in a contest, which deserve delicate design.

②Theme tourism

Theme tourism, a current popular travel product, is a good weapon to fight in such a speech competition. It refers to in-depth understanding and experience of a certain topic or a certain destination. As an upgraded version of traditional mass tourism, the tourism routes are always tailored for tourists based on their different identities, personal needs, unique experiences and consumption psychology.

The following themes are popular in modern tourism industry.

a. Ecotourism (eco-travel, ecological tourism)

b. Extreme tourism (yacht, rafting, skiing, hiking)

c. Soul, pilgrimage

d. Parent-child

e. Agritainment (happy farmhouse)

f. Study tour

g. Photography

More specific and innovative themes are there. It will be more creative and refreshing if your team works out an original and extraordinary theme. We highly recommend planning a tour around a theme. In this way, the destination satisfying your need will emerge easily, as well as activities, scenic spots and so on. These stuff can be closely related and connected and the theme could stand out benefiting this design.

③What sceneries are we going to admire?

Think about our focus in the tour product prior to deciding what places of interest or sceneries to visit. The following questions will help your team design a wonderful tour plan.

a. What do they prefer to admire? Natural beauty, culture, history, art or architecture?

b. What do we want our tourists to get? For instance, spiritual or material?

a)Can they broaden their horizon through seeing those natural wonders or absorbing more knowledge in the aspects of history, science or art?

b)Can they remember what's there in the destination when they leave?

c)If it is material, what can they take away?

c. Do they expect a peaceful journey or an exciting adventure?

What feeling do you expect those tourists to have in your desgin? Excited, surprised or refreshed?

Traditionally, we can divide those tourist attractions or say scenic spots according to tourism resources into human landscape resources, folk customs resources, traditional food resources, cultural and art resources, crafts resources, and urban and pastoral scenery resources. We think about what we mainly do, and then do some research on some cities or towns, which can meet all the requirements. Those activities you plan to carry out in the destination are around the theme you plan in advance.

4. Design a route/itinerary

With a certain destination and exact theme, it's time for us to design the route and itinerary. When we design the itinerary, we must cover the main elements in our plan as follows.

a. Are activities and tourism attractions relevant to the theme?

b. Is transportation available there?

c. Is the travel time short or acceptable as the instruction requires?

（二）Features of customers

As we mentioned above, to work out a wonderful tour plan, thinking about features of customers and their needs thoroughly is a must. We list several issues worth of meditation as follows.

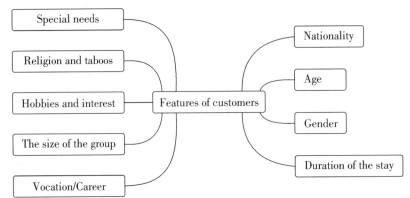

Nationality

People from different countries have their own customs and living habits, which yearn for your research. Making a connection or correlation between your tour introduction and their background can double the effect of the plan. For example, people from Australia are also called KIWI, which can be joined to the fruit kiwi, a native plant in Hunan, China.

Age

Fully consider about tourists' age, because people at different age have their unique needs such as suitable amount of physical activities for senior citizens. With this consideration, the tour product would be more reasonable and considerate.

Gender

Customize some activities corresponding to the gender if the group consists of all males or all females, or one side prevailing in number.

Vocation/Career

Sometimes, the trip could be a business trip or a trip for inspiration. If your tourists are computer engineers, it would be a good idea for them to stay in a rural area to escape from big burden of coding and programming. Visiting an exhibition of digital products could also be a good choice for this group.

Hobbies or interest

It would be definitely welcome if your tour plan covered tourists' favourite activities or events, which made the tour plan outstand from the ordinary with great attraction and joy.

The size of the group

The number of tourists determines the activity type and the time spent on each activity. If it is a small group, a tour guide may be able to offer a more profound and thorough introduction about some places of interest to tourists.

Duration of the stay

This weighs much in deciding how many places to go and what vehicles to take to realize the tour plan.

Religion and taboos

Respect their religions and taboos, and avoid designing speeches or activities which may offend them. It couldn't be more inappropriate than taking Muslims to worship Buddhas.

Special needs

Usually, in the instruction of the speech competition, special needs might be mentioned. This deserves the most attention in such a competition.

（三）Part 2　Tour guide

Tour guides' attitudes tell guests whether they take the job seriously, reflect their professional quality and also determine guests' views on their service.

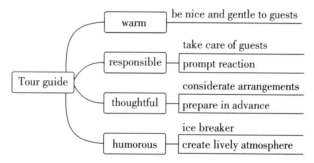

1. Abilities

Tour guides are required to ensure the safety of the whole group, keep the tour going according to the itinerary, and introduce local attractions to guests. To some extent, tour guides need to be well-rounded.

2. Good communication skills

How to introduce yourself and leave a good impression? How to greet guests and create active atmosphere? How to explain and comfort guests when incidents occur? How to solve problems without irritating guests?

Proper interpersonal skills may be the answer to all these questions. Think about this situation: your guests are not allowed to climb mountains due to bad weather, thus feeling really disappointed and complaining a lot. What should you say?

Here are two examples:

A	Please stop blaming me! It's not my fault! You know the weather is changeable during this time of the year. Do you really want to risk your lives to go up there? I don't!
B	I totally understand how you feel rightnow, and I'm terribly sorry for the unexpected situation. We'll climb the mountain tomorrow if the weather permits, or I'll lead you to visit a national park for free as compensation.

Obviously, B is much better than A, which may drive guests crazy. Guide B offers a sincere apology and reasonable compensation, and shows her understanding of guests' unpleasant feelings, thus Guide B will probably calm them down and achieve a satisfactory result.

Last but not least, a bilingual tour guide must speak a fluent foreign language, which is English in many cases, and be familiar with daily expressions.

3. Wide cultural knowledge

To introduce Chinese culture in a vivid way and enhance guests' understanding of this long-history country, a tour guide must be an expert in many aspects, including art, architecture, instruments, cuisine and so on.

In addition, you should analyze guests' backgrounds and try to overcome cultural barriers. Avoid discussing sensitive topics like religion, political views, which may lead to a bitter dispute and cause conflict.

4. Strong safety awareness

Security is always the first priority. Take any possible danger into consideration when you plan the trip, make full preparations to avoid it, and take immediate actions when it occurs.

An experienced tour guide must be fully alert to potential risks, have the capacity to deal with emergencies thoroughly and reduce loss to the smallest degree.

5. Duties

Having designed a tour plan for your guests and confirmed their arriving time, you're going to pick them up at the airport, high-speed train station or any other appointed places.

A friendly greeting and a warm welcome speech will win your guests' reliance and make a good debut of the tour.

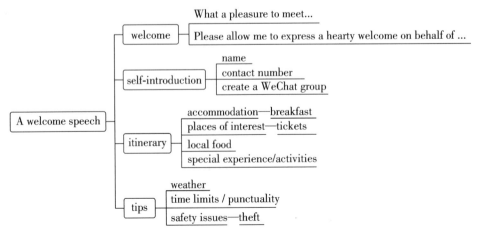

While travelling, you should always be alert and ready to deal with unexpected situations. Safety always comes first, and emergencies may occur.

Tour guides should remind guests of potential risks at the very beginning and take prompt actions when meeting trouble. For instance, in case of injuries, a tour guide should remind guests of dangers in advance, like the slippery floor, not to take photos while walking, check the wound and provide first aid immediately, calm down the injured guest and ask others to stay in place, call 120 and accompany the patient to the hospital if necessary. Make sincere apologies and offer compensation to make up for the inconvenience caused to your guests.

In addition, it's crucial to keep the tour going as planned. Never change the itinerary unless something unusual happens. As we mentioned before, the judge raises a question "What measures will you take if we miss the train?", and the tour guide may suggest changing the destination due to time limited, but in most cases, it's not a good choice and won't be accepted by guests.

6. Values

Although the tour guide needs to take care of all guests and shoulder great responsibilities during the trip, it is undeniable that this job has considerable merits as follows:

- Enrich social/academic/professional experience.
- First-hand experience / multi-sensory experience.
- Broaden one's horizons/visions.
- Relax one's body and ease one's mind.
- Promote cultural communication and interaction with locals / people of different backgrounds.
- Acquire knowledge about old buildings of special aesthetic value.
- …

（四）Vocabulary list for this module

responsible 负责的；可靠的；有责任的
bilingual 双语的
fluent 流畅的；流利的
taboo 禁忌；禁止
barrier 障碍物；屏障；界线
religion 宗教；宗教信仰
marital status 婚姻状况
emergency 紧急情况；突发事件；非常时刻
awareness 意识；认识；明白；知道
slippery 滑的
multi-sensory 多感官的
accompany 陪伴；伴随
inconvenience 不便；麻烦
interaction 相互作用；相互影响；交流
aesthetic 美的；美学的；审美的；有审美观点的
travel agency 旅行社
travel agent 旅行代办人
schedule 时间表；日程表
route 路线
itinerary 行程路线
strategy 策略；方法
exhibition 展览
fee 费用
fare 门票；车票
nationality 国籍
hospitality 款待；好客
sustainability 可持续性

transportation 交通
vehicle 交通工具
gender 性别
accommodation 食宿；住宿
luxury 奢华的；豪华的
deluxe 豪华的
resort 度假胜地
hostel 宿舍；临时收容所
inn 小旅馆；小酒店
motel 汽车旅馆
lounge 休息室；等候室
lobby 大厅；大堂
front desk 前台；迎宾台
twin room 双人间
suite 套房；包间
express 快捷酒店
check in 入住；登记
check out 退房；迁出
register 注册；登记
credit 信用卡
payment 支付方式
deposit 押金；存款
shuttle bus 区间车；通行巴士
client 客户；客人
reservation 预约；预订
sightseeing 观光
cuisine 菜系；风味

第二节　思维训练

一、Mind map

通过前一节专业知识的学习，我们已经对商业和旅游方面的知识有了大致了解。下面我们通过思维导图的方式，迅速复习相关专业知识，并且训练选手的发散思维，从而 A 选手能更好地撰写 A 稿，B 选手能更有针对性地回答相关问题。

（一）What are the essential qualities for a sales person?

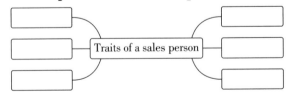

Possible answer:

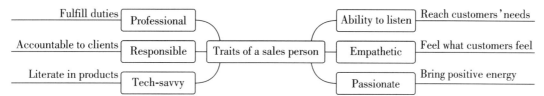

（二）Can you elaborate the after-sales procedure for me?

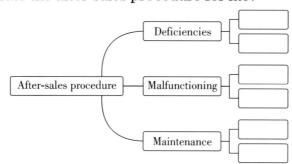

Possible answer:

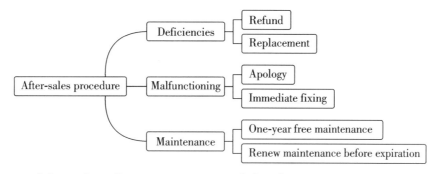

（三）How would you handle customer complaints?

Possible answer:

（四）Can you list some advantages of online selling?

Possible answer:

（五）How about your company's future developing/five-year plan?

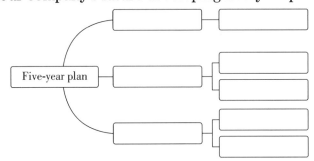

Possible answer：

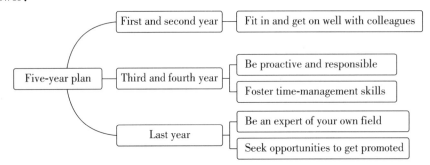

（六）What can you do to attract more customers?

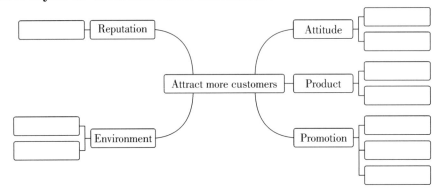

Possible answer:

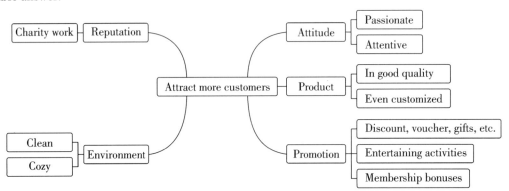

（七）How to enhance the service?

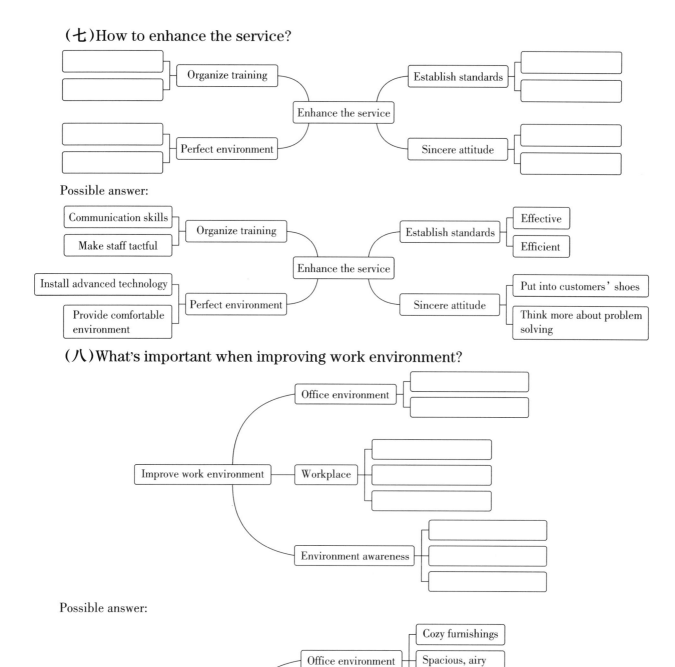

Possible answer:

（八）What's important when improving work environment?

（九）Why is employee training program important for a company?

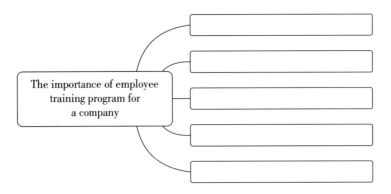

Possible answer:

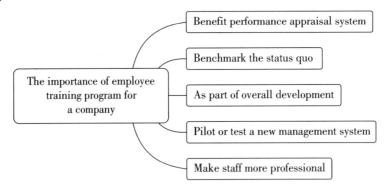

（十）How does the Internet influence service industries?

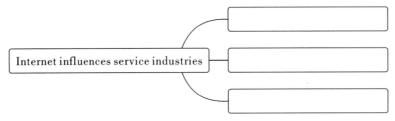

Possible answer:

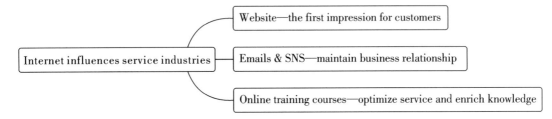

（十一）Why do you choose xxx (city name) as your destination?

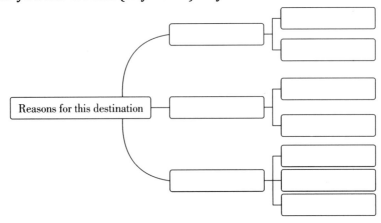

Possible answer:

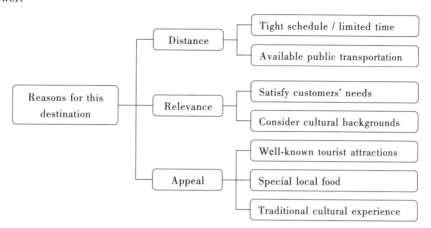

（十二）What features have you taken into consideration when planning the tour?

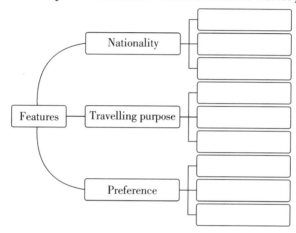

Possible answer:

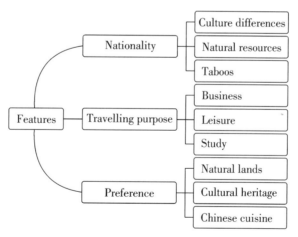

（十三）How would you overcome the language barrier?

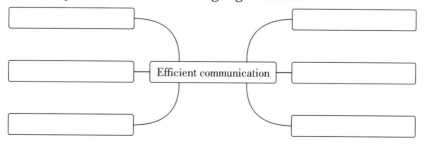

Possible answer:

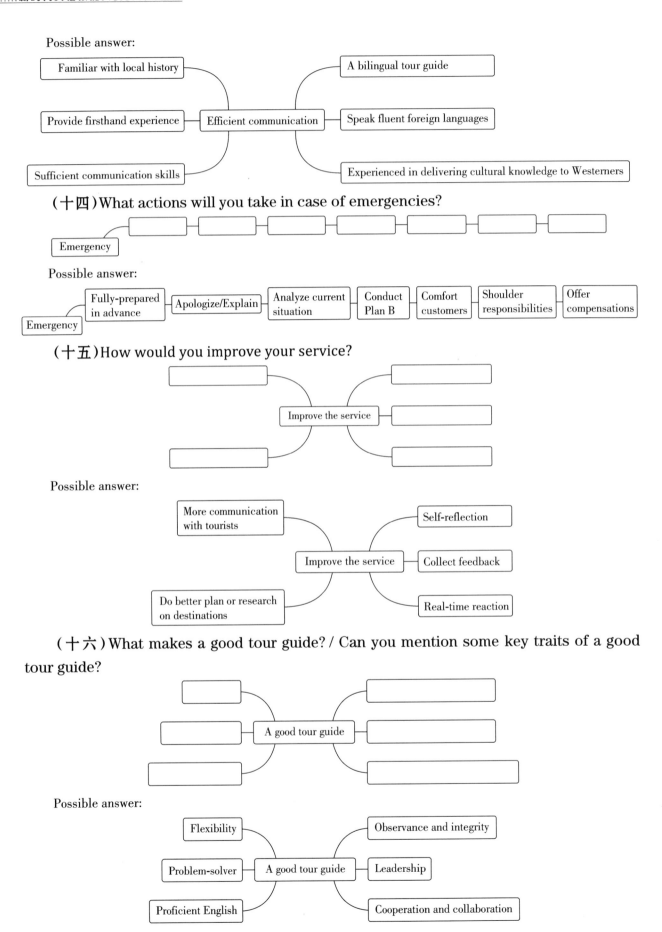

Familiar with local history

A bilingual tour guide

Provide firsthand experience — Efficient communication — Speak fluent foreign languages

Sufficient communication skills

Experienced in delivering cultural knowledge to Westerners

（十四）What actions will you take in case of emergencies?

Emergency

Possible answer:

Emergency — Fully-prepared in advance — Apologize/Explain — Analyze current situation — Conduct Plan B — Comfort customers — Shoulder responsibilities — Offer compensations

（十五）How would you improve your service?

Improve the service

Possible answer:

More communication with tourists

Self-reflection

Improve the service — Collect feedback

Do better plan or research on destinations

Real-time reaction

（十六）What makes a good tour guide? / Can you mention some key traits of a good tour guide?

A good tour guide

Possible answer:

Flexibility

Observance and integrity

Problem-solver — A good tour guide — Leadership

Proficient English

Cooperation and collaboration

（十七）If the guests choose to do some exploration on their own, what should the tour guide do?

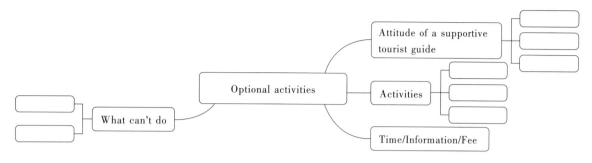

Possible answer:

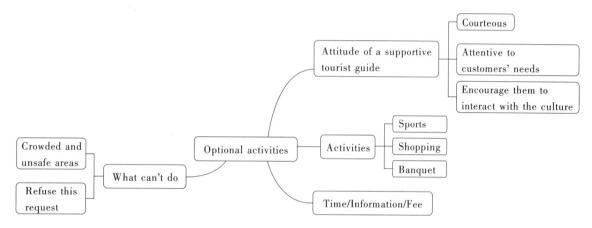

（十八）What consideration do you make for your tourists' identity as businessmen?

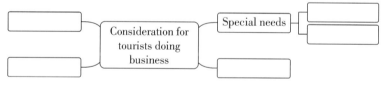

Possible answer:

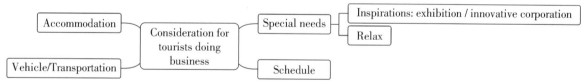

（十九）What will a tour guide suggest tourists to bring before the trip?

Possible answer:

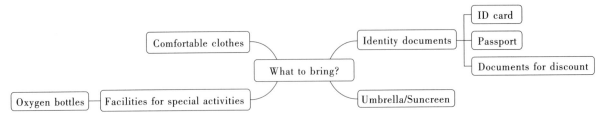

（二十）Can tour guides play jokes to activate the atmosphere?

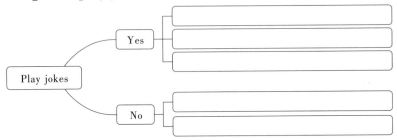

Possible answer:

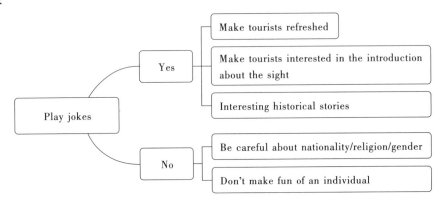

二、Match

笔试中关于职业描述与职业匹配题旨在考查选手对各类职业的理解与职场应用。我们发现,选手在这类题目上往往失分较多。所以,在训练期间,职业词汇以及职业的基础内容的介绍能帮助选手在口试中高水平发挥。

（一）Exercise 1

No.	Answer	Job	Job Description
1		Chemist	A. People who study humans, animals, plants and bacteria to gain a better understanding of how the body and nature work
2		Biologist	B. A person engaged in chemical research or experiments
3		Psychologist	C. A person whose job is to take care of sick or injured people, usually in a hospital
4		Therapist	D. A licensed expert that is able to practice diagnosis, treatment and other related services on your teeth
5		Dentist	E. An expert who can deliver satisfactory translation service either in a written or oral form to its targeted customers

No.	Answer	Job	Job Description
6		Professor	F. A person who specializes in the study of mind and behavior or in the treatment of mental, emotional, and behavioral disorders
7		Doctor	G. A person who studies human history and prehistory through the excavation of sites and the analysis of artifacts and other physical remains
8		Nurse	H. Someone who explores and identifies the basic principles that govern the structure and behaviour of matter, the interaction between energy and matter, and the generation and transfer of energy
9		Curator	I. People who have passion and thirst for numbers, willing to make discoveries in the field of equation, algebra and geometry
10		Interpreter	J. A person licensed to practice medicine, as a physician, surgeon, dentist, or veterinarian
11		Author	K. A green hand who is learning a trade from a skilled employer, having agreed to work for a fixed period at low wages
12		Apprentice	L. A person who treats mental illness by discussing somebody's problems with them through special treatment rather than by giving them drugs or diagnosis
13		Physicist	M. A university teacher of the highest rank
14		Mathematician	N. A person whose job is to be in charge of the objects or works of art in a museum or an art gallery
15		Archeologist	O. A person who writes books, articles or plays, etc.

Key: 1-5 BAFLD   6-10 MJCNE   11-15 OKHIG

(二)Exercise 2

No.	Answer	Job	Job Description
1		Barber /Hairdresser	A. A person or company who involves in trade, especially dealing import and export business
2		Bartender	B. A second-year student in university
3		Musician	C. A person with a medical degree whose job is to treat people who are ill or hurt
4		Merchant	D. A man who has never married
5		Magician	E. A person who performs magic tricks for entertainment
6		Freshman	F. A person who plays a musical instrument or is musically talented
7		Sophomore	G. A first-year student in university
8		Junior	H. A person who is very skilled in a job or some area
9		Senior	I. A student at a college or university who has not yet earned a bachelor's or an equivalent degree
10		Master	J. A person who cuts or styles hair

续 表

No.	Answer	Job	Job Description
11		Doctor	K. A person who keeps or inspects financial accounts
12		Bachelor	L. A fourth-year student in university
13		Undergraduate	M. A student engaged in postgraduate courses of study
14		Postgraduate	N. A third-year student in university
15		Accountant	O. A person who serves drinks at a bar

Key: 1-5 JOFAE   6-10 GBNLH   11-15 CDIMK

(三)Exercise 3

No.	Answer	Job	Job Description
1		Engineer	A. A person who is trained for travelling in a spacecraft
2		Astronaut	B. A person who designs new buildings and makes certain that they are built correctly
3		Pilot	C. A person whose job is to design things by making drawings of them
4		Pharmacist	D. A person who is employed to clean the rooms and furniture inside a building
5		Handyman	E. An employee of a bank who receives and pays out money
6		Designer	F. A person who is trained to fly an aircraft
7		Chef	G. A person whose job is to study companies' financial performance, usually in order to decide which ones to invest in
8		Cleaner	H. A person who writes news stories or articles for a newspaper or magazine or broadcasts them on radio or television
9		Bank clerk	I. A man who works on a ship, plane, or train, taking care of passengers and serving meals to them
10		Declarant	J. A person who uses scientific knowledge to design, construct, and maintain engines and machines or structures such as roads, railroads, and bridges
11		Stockbroker	K. A cook in a restaurant or hotel
12		Financial analyst	L. A person who makes or signs a statement that declares that the information given is true
13		Architect	M. A man who earns money by doing small jobs for people such as making and repairing things in their houses
14		Steward	N. A person whose job is to buy and sell stocks and shares for people who want to invest money
15		Journalist	O. A person who is qualified to prepare and sell medicines

Key: 1-5 JAFOM   6-10 CKDEL   11-15 NGBIH

（四）Exercise 4

No.	Answer	Job	Job Description
1		Civil servant	A. A person whose job is to stop fires from burning
2		Tour guide	B. A person who works in a place such as a hotel, office, or hospital, who welcomes and helps visitors and answers the phone
3		Firefighter	C. A person whose job is to receive and pay out money in a shop, bank, restaurant, etc.
4		Receptionist	D. A person whose job is to supply and connect or repair water pipes, baths, toilets, etc.
5		Operator	E. A person who works in a government department responsible for putting central government plans into action.
6		Cashier	F. A person who works in an office, writing letters, making phone calls, and arranging meetings for a person or for an organization
7		Deliveryman	G. People who actually carry out the blueprint done architect and mainly do the work of building or making something, especially buildings, bridges, etc.
8		Waiter	H. A person whose job is making and repairing wooden objects and structures
9		Assistant	I. A person whose job is to bring the food to customers at their tables in a restaurant
10		Carpenter	J. A person who is responsible for managing a hotel, hospitality service, catering service and so on
11		Hotel manager	K. Someone who helps someone else to do a job
12		Construction worker	L. A person offers tour service such as guiding the way, giving introduction about scenic spots and offering the proper itinerary
13		Plumber	M. A person prevents people going into places without permission, transporting large amounts of money, or protecting goods from being stolen
14		Secretary	N. A man who delivers goods to people's houses or places of work
15		Security guard	O. A person who uses and controls a machine or vehicle

Keys: 1-5 ELABO   6-10 CNIKH   11-15 JGDFM

三、B选手快问快答

根据之前的章节，我们依托宁波市2018年和2019年两届市赛的第二环节主题产品营销的题目，为B选手的现场问答环节延展了近百道题目。下面是我们斟酌挑选后，较有代表性的20道问题以及我们的相应回答。读者可以根据我们给的题目寻找解题思路，准备自己的应对方案。

1. What aspects of your products that you think can be improved?

There is no perfect product since human beings ever started developing goods, and our product is no exception. In order to satisfy the middle and higher income customers within the market, we choose to get rid of some personalized features to meet the needs of working class. However, in the future, we will always stay committed to innovating our technology and enhancing craftsmanship, thus providing our customers with the best user experience.

However, with the popularization of intelligent technology, our products are more likely to reach every class of our society, therefore bringing green life to every home.

2. What is your pricing strategy/tactics?

We sell our products at a price of 999 pounds which is based on a comprehensive market research conducted throughout the European market. Our major competitors priced their products within the range of 600 to 800 pounds by satisfying their customers with ordinary functions, however, our product outshines our rivals in the following aspects, the value of sustainable life, the smart expiry date alert function as well as the customized services. Besides, the price achieves sufficient profit margin to cover research and development expenditure(R&D costs), and also allows us to strike a balance between input and output.

3. How would you resolve after-sales problems?

Once our customers filed an after-sales problem either online or offline, we will immediately initiate our problem-dealing mechanism in order to tackle the problem and maintain company image. First, we will express our sincere apologies for their unpleasant shopping experience. Second, a comprehensive research into the malfunctioning problem will be conducted so as to provide a detailed and reasonable report to our customers whether this problem had been triggered by wrongful procedures or product failure which will help us to further improve our craft. Lastly, we will either provide our customers with a refund or replacement on the condition that it is our responsibility.

4. How to promote your product?

A comprehensive promotion plan that combines online and offline promotion is of paramount importance when it comes to advertising. Speaking of the offline promotion, we will resort to the help of roadshows and experience stores that can best showcase our products to the customers and optimize customers' user experience that can increase the possibility of purchasing to some extent. As of online advertising, taking advantage of celebrity economy is an efficient way to introduce products into different segments, which can be both labor and money saving as people nowadays are likely to be influenced by the celebrity economy.

5. How to develop customers' loyalty?

Developing loyal customers is beneficial to the long-term development of the company.

Firstly, maintain the good business relation with customers, make regular follow-up visits to old customers and stay active in front of them so that they will think about you for the next cooperation.

Secondly, pay attention to customers' feedback, listen to their suggestions with an open mind and keep optimizing products so as to win their loyalty.

What's more, offering a wonderful after-sales service can greatly enhance the customers' goodwill to us.

6. Who is your potential customer / target market?

Firstly, we lean to white-collars who are always busy at work and have no time to consume the food in the refrigerator, which will lead to food expiration and unnecessary waste.

Secondly, middle and higher income families are our choices. In light of our innovative technology and creative design, our pricing covers business cooperation fee, research and development expenditure and so on, which take a great deal of efforts and human resources, therefore these two kinds of families may find the price reasonable and practical.

Thirdly, for people who are concerned about green-house effect and want a sustainable life, our ECO fridge can give them wonderful user experience.

7. What are good qualities of being a good salesperson?

Firstly, I think friendliness and approachability are useful traits in terms of conducting business. Salespeople should have a neat and pleasant appearance that projects confidence and willingness to help customers, and make customers feel more comfortable to ask questions and get assistance.

Secondly, being able to quickly adapt to changing environment and conditions is also a valuable merit. As long as you can properly handle the upcoming issues at work, you will always find yourself invincible in the field of marketing.

What's more, communication skills and a broad knowledge are prerequisites for being a good salesman.

8. How can you dominate the market share / outshine in the market? =How to convince your customers to buy your product? =What is the strength of your product?

Firstly, every item's expiry date will be spontaneously recorded in scanning function, thus contributing to live an eco-friendly life.

Plus, our customized recipes will be formed according to the personal health data collected by the system so that people no longer have to worry about the obesity and diabetes because they are eating the most ideal dietary choice provided by our ECO fridge. Moreover, hating to get out the bed during weekend, our ECO fridge is smart enough to automatically send the food supply request according to your eating habits which can save you a great deal of time.

Anyway, all these outstanding features of our ECO fridge will be sure to outperform all competitors in the market.

9. Can you name some barriers or difficulties for salespeople?

The moment you decided to become a professional salesperson, the moment you should determine your goal and be prepared for upcoming challenges.

Firstly, excessive competition is commonly seen in everyday selling scenario, and fierce competition will not only steal the confidence of salespeople but also strengthen their belief to quit.

Secondly, salespeople may experience dismay or psychological trauma when being rejected or turned down by their customers, which may potentially hurt their pride or discourage them from engaging in this field.

Lastly, little interest and feedback from customers can also frustrate salespersons' enthusiasm that may make it harder for them to keep their work going.

10. How will your product transform the way that people live?

I believe our fit mask will profoundly change the way that we live in the following aspects. Firstly, people no longer have to bother about degraded air quality issue since fit mask can provide them with 24 hours protection. What's more, facial recognition system can tremendously reduce the time wasted on mask-wearing and give timely health report to our users. Last but not least, TCM tonics can not only contribute to our respiratory system but also can calm down our spirit, which in turn can spread the greatness of TCM.

11. Why do you choose Jinan as your destination?

First, considering customers' requirements about high speed train and their tight business schedule, Jinan came in our mind due to the short distance within 2 hours from Beijing.

Second, Jinan's unique natural spring wonders and its spring culture, history and food make it distinguished, and this non-material heritage makes an analogy to New Zealand for both having rich water resources.

We believe our friends will find the correlation with Jinan and experience novelty when exploring this Spring City.

12. What is the highlight of your tourism product?

The unique spring culture and various activities related to this theme make our trip outshine the others. By sipping spring tea, admiring traditional architectures built around springs, playing spring-themed games, enjoying local spring dishes, our guests can experience the past and future of the spring culture, thus kindling the passion, getting involved, wandering around historic sites, and interacting with the vivid history. That's our specially tailored KIWI trip for Kiwis.

13. What cultural features have you considered when designing the tour for New Zealanders?

We've searched a lot of information to be fully prepared. First, New Zealand is a multicultural country with people from diverse backgrounds, and our guests are curious about Chinese culture and history, so we lead them to explore the unique spring culture. Second, New Zealanders enjoy a slow-pace and relaxing lifestyle, so we offer them a carefree tour with entertaining activities, like sipping spring tea and admiring sceneries by boat. Third, New Zealanders love drinking tea and prefer light and fresh food, so we take them to have a bite of spring banquet, which contains local fresh ingredients.

14. How do you solve the problem they may not quite understand Chinese?/ How do you make your communication with these New Zealanders efficient?/ How do you make your message get through your guests?

Actually, the language barrier won't be a problem. We two, as bilingual tour guides, can speak fluent English and communicate smoothly with our guests. Besides, we are experienced in leading tours with Western travelers, knowing how to deliver cultural knowledge in an easily understandable way. Thirdly, we are familiar with the local life and history, thus providing firsthand experience for our guests to feel what spring cultural life is like in China.

15. Do you think your trip is perfect?

Considering feasibility and meaning of our tour, we're quite satisfied with it, since we provide multisensory experience within a short time and also ensure that our guests won't feel tired. However, nothing is perfect. If given more time, we could lead guests to further explore splendid culture and history in Jinan. For instance, we could go to Thousand Buddha Mountain to seek more springs, have an insight into Buddhist culture and retrieve inner-peace.

16. How would you deal with complaints?

First and foremost, we need to calm down customers, talk to them in time and ease their mood. Then we'll figure out why they complained and offer solutions. The reason may vary, terrible food, bad weather, uncomfortable hotels could all be a trigger. Once we know what happened, immediate actions are taken to solve the problem. For instance, we may lead them to a better restaurant or provide food that suits their taste. In addition, we could offer some compensation, like souvenirs or vouchers, to make up for our mistake and express our sincere apology.

17. What actions will you take in case of emergencies?

As qualified tour guides, we receive professional training once a month and are well-prepared to deal with emergencies properly. We'll follow emergency response procedures, analyze the situation and take corresponding actions. For instance, if someone is injured, we'll give him first-aid, stop bleeding, call the ambulance and send him to hospital. Then we'll comfort other customers, bring them to a safe place, contact our travel agency and report the accident to the police if necessary.

18. What would you do to break the ice and put your guests at ease at the beginning of the tour?

First impressions are the most lasting. We'll give customers a warm greeting and appealing self-introduction to create active atmosphere and make them feel relaxed. Tell some jokes about places of interest to draw their attention, lead in the itinerary smoothly and explain the route of the day. After that, we may invite customers to introduce themselves in turns to get familiar with each other, and distribute tailored wristbands or caps to build a sense of belonging.

19. How would you improve your tour service?

First of all, we will explore more places and activities which could bring refreshed and novel experience to our tourists. Also, we belive a deep perspective to narrate a story or to introduce a historical sight weighs much when continuously attracting and impressing tourists. Last but not least, good communication must be carried out before, during and after the trip. That could help us better understand the merits and flaws in our tourism product and make adjustments to better the service.

20. If your guests are curious about some sensitive topics, e.g. Hong Kong, and want to discuss with you, what would you do?

First, I realize this topic is not easy to talk about with strangers, because you don't know their political stance in those sensitive topics. What I say is highly possible offensive to them, although they may encourage you to say whatever you like. Also, when we talk about this as a tour guide in a tour, the words I say are no more individual opinions but in half of an organization or bigger. Therefore, I will first show my respect and admiration that they are sensitive to those latest news, then I will state that I'm not familiar or not so sure of these topics, avoiding giving opinions or talks on those issues. Instead I will say, "Please allow me to read more and watch more, I will not talk about it until I fully understand the situation."

第四章 模拟试题

第一节 环节一 笔试

试题(一)

本次考试包括听力和阅读两部分,共55道题目。请在1小时之内完成。

听力测试现在开始。

Part I Listening 听力(20%)

Section A (10%)

In this section, you will hear 10 short dialogues and questions. There are three pictures marked A, B, and C for each question. Choose the one that best matches the question. Each dialogue and question will be read just once and you will have 15 seconds for each question.(在本节中,你将听到10个短对话和相应的问题。每道题配有A、B、C三幅图片,选出与题目内容相符合的一幅图片。每个对话和问题读一遍,每题你有15秒钟的作答时间。)

( )1. What does the man want?

A.　　　　　　　　
B.　　　　　　　　C.

( )2. What's the woman's job?

A.　　　　　　　　
B.　　　　　　　　
C.

( )3. Which language does the woman know a little?

A.　　　　　　　　
B.　　　　　　　　
C.

( )4. What did the man want?

- 62 -

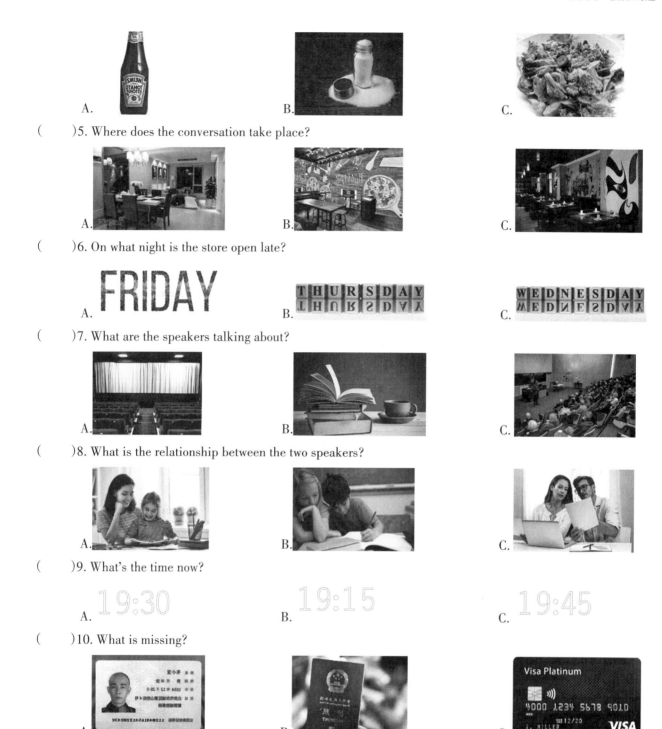

A. B. C.

(　　)5. Where does the conversation take place?

A. B. C.

(　　)6. On what night is the store open late?

A. B. C.

(　　)7. What are the speakers talking about?

A. B. C.

(　　)8. What is the relationship between the two speakers?

A. B. C.

(　　)9. What's the time now?

A. B. C.

(　　)10. What is missing?

A. B. C.

Section B (5%)

In this section, you will hear a dialogue. After the dialogue, five questions will be asked. There are three choices marked A, B, and C for each question. Choose the one that best answers the question. The dialogue and questions will be read just once and you will have 15 seconds for each question.(在本节中,你将听到 1 段对话和 5 个相应的问题。每道题配有 A、B、C 三个选项,选出与题目内容相符的一个答案。对话和每个问题读一遍,每题你有 15 秒钟的作答时间。)

(　　)11. Michelle is _____.

A. the job interviewer   B. the job interviewee   C. the new secretary

(   )12. Where are the two speakers?

A. In an office.   B. In a hotel.   C. In a shop.

(   )13. What language can Michelle speak?

A. Italian.   B. Spanish.   C. French.

(   )14. One of Michelle's job duties is to _____.

A. clean desks   B. write reports   C. take care of children

(   )15. Which of the following statements is TRUE?

A. Claire wants a secretary for four days a week.

B. Michelle can't use a computer.

C. Michelle can't work for Claire at weekends.

Section C (5%)

In this section, you will hear a dialogue. After the dialogue, arrange the following activities in the correct order.（在本节中，你将听到1段对话。根据对话中的内容将下列活动排序。）

| A. read newspapers | B. go for a walk with a dog | C. speak to the assistant |
| D. go to work | E. have dinner | |

16._____   17._____   18._____   19._____   20._____

Part II   Reading 阅读（80%）

Section A (20%)

In this section, you will read 20 short dialogues or pictures. Choose from A, B, and C the choice that best completes the dialogue, sentence or answers the question.（在本节中，你将读到20个短对话或图片，从A、B、C三个选项中选出能够补全对话、句子或回答问题的最恰当的选项。）

(   )21. —What are you going to do this weekend?

—_____. If time permits, I may go to Shanghai with my friends.

A. Don't mention it   B. It doesn't matter   C. Forget it   D. It depends

(   )22. —Don't worry, Mum. The doctor said it was only the flu.

—_____! I'll tell Dad there's nothing serious.

A. What a relief   B. Congratulations   C. How surprising   D. I'm so sorry

(   )23. —Honey, the cat's stuck in the tree.

—Can you turn off the TV and get a ladder?

—Oh, it jumped off. _____.

A. Never mind   B. All right   C. No problem   D. Take care

(   )24. —Have you paid? What's my share of the bill?

—_____. It wasn't very much.

A. Don't worry about it B. It's my share   C. None of your business   D. It's up to you

(   )25. —I'm terribly sorry to interrupt, but may I use your phone? It's rather urgent.

—Yes, _____.

    A. with pleasure   B. no hurry   C. it doesn't matter   D. of course

(　　)26. —What shall we do tonight then?

    — _____. Whatever you want.

    A. Help yourself   B. It's a deal   C. No problem   D. It's up to you

(　　)27. —Try not to work yourself too hard. Take it easy.

    —Thanks. _____

    A. So what?   B. No way.   C. What for?   D. You, too.

(　　)28. —Sorry I'm late. I got stuck in traffic.

    — _____. You're here now. Come in and sit down.

    A. You are welcome   B. That's right   C. I have no idea   D. Never mind

(　　)29. —I'm sorry for being late. I should have phoned you earlier.

    — _____. I've just arrived.

    A. That's no trouble   B. You are welcome   C. That's all right   D. You can never tell

(　　)30. —The trip shouldn't take more than an hour.

    — _____. It is at least two hours.

    A. I guess so   B. That's it   C. You must be joking   D. It depends

(　　)31. —Excuse me. How much is the shirt?

    — _____.

    A. Extra large   B. 50 yuan each   C. It sells well   D. Altogether there are 5

(　　)32. —Can I have a day off tomorrow, Mr Johnson?

    — _____. I can manage without you.

    A. Forget it   B. I'm afraid not   C. It depends   D. Of course

(　　)33. —You have to believe in yourself. No one else will, if you don't.

    — _____. Confidence is really important.

    A. It's not my cup of tea   B. That's not the point   C. I don't think so   D. I couldn't agree more

(　　)34. —Is there anything else to discuss?

    — _____. I guess.

    A. Not at all   B. No, that's all   C. Yes, I'm sure   D. Yes, of course

(　　)35. —I'm going to San Francisco for a couple of days.

    — _____. I wish I could get away for a while.

    A. It doesn't matter   B. Forget it   C. I really envy you   D. I can't agree more

(　　)36. —Look, here comes your dream girl. Invite her to dance.

    — _____ What if she refuses me?

    A. I don't know.   B. Why me?   C. With pleasure.   D. So what?

(　　)37. —May I help you? You seem to be having some problems.

    — _____, thanks. I think I can manage.

    A. All right   B. No problem   C. It's all right   D. There's no way

(　　)38. —I love the Internet. I've come to know many friends on the Net.

— _____. Few of them would become your real friends.

　　　　A. That's for sure　B. It's not the case　　　C. I couldn't agree more　D. I'm pleased to know that

(　　)39. —The Modern Art Exhibition in the City Museum has been cancelled.

　　　　—Oh, no!_____.

　　　　A. It's a pity　　　B. It doesn't matter　　　C. I knew it already　　　D. It's not interesting at all

(　　)40. —Which one of these do you want?

　　　　— _____. Either will do.

　　　　A. I don't mind　　B. I'm sure　　　　　C. No problem　　　　D. Go ahead

Section B (10%)

In this section, you will read 2 dialogues. For each blank, choose from A, B, C, D, and E the expression that best completes the dialogue. （在本节中，你将读到2段对话。从 A、B、C、D、E 五个选项中选出能够补全对话的最恰当的选项。）

Dialogue 1

A. sign here	B. fill in this form	C. have a reservation
D. By visa	E. Just a moment	

A: Good evening. What can I do for you?

B: Hello, I'd like to check in.

A: Did you _____41_____?

B: Yes, Chen XX, from tonight to the 31st, three nights. Here's my ID card.

A: _____42_____, please. I'll check the reservation record.

…

A: Sorry to keep you waiting. It's a standard business room, right?

B: Yeah.

A: Could you please_____43_____?

B: Fine.

A: How would you like to pay?

B: _____44_____. Here it is.

A: OK. Please key in your password.

…

A: Thank you, please_____45_____. Your room number is 8201, on the second floor.

B: Thank you.

Dialogue 2

A. book the tickets	B. schedule	C. Round trip
D. by card	E. nonstop flight	

A: Hello, I need to _____46_____ my trip to Hong Kong for next week.

B: When would you like to travel?

A: I have to reach Hong Kong by the 19th.

B: Is this a _____47_____? Will you need a return ticket, too?

A: Yes, check that for the 26th in the evening.

B: Yes, there's a _____48_____ to Hong Kong from LHR Airport at 9 p.m. on the 19th. On the 26th you may board Flight VS207, which is also nonstop at 11:55 p.m.

A: Okay, fine.

B: Would you like to _____49_____ then?

A: What's the cost?

B: That will be 7,838 yuan.

A: I will pay _____50_____.

Section C (10%)

The following chart shows a STORE DIRECTORY. Decide which section each person needs to shop. (下面表格是一份商场指南。请根据客户需求将他们匹配到他们的目标楼层。)

A. Banking	
ANZ Bank	LG S8
Australia Post	L1 S7
B. Hair & Beauty	
Just Cuts	L2 S9
Jade Hair Designs	L2 S8
C. Fashion & Accessories	
Jeans West	L1 S6
Scarves For You	L1 S10
D. Food Court	
Donut King	LG S2
Sunshine Sushi	LG S4
E. Gifts and Books	
Dymocks	L2 S3
Lego	L2 S1
F. Chemists	
Priceline	L1 S4
G. Homeware	
Hani Homeware	L1 S14
H. Electrical, Music & Games	
JB Hi Fi	L2 S8
Sam's Electrics	LG S5
I. Jewellery	
Proud's	L1 S15
J. Liquor	
Liquorland	L1 S1
K. Children's Wear	
Cotton Kids	L1 S9
L. Supermarkets	
Woolworhs	LG S11

(　　)51. Lee and his fiancée are preparing for their engagement and they are searching for a private hair designer.

(　　)52. Miss Zhang, a secretary of a multinational company, is preparing refreshments for the year-end party.

(　　)53. Annie, from the department of purchasing, is preparing gifts for the year-end party. She knows many of the male colleagues prefer alcohol.

(　　)54. Chef Jeremy is preparing the year-end dinner and he wants to purchase all the ingredients by himself.

(　　)55. Mike is preparing for the financial report and he is going to fetch the bank reconciliation.

(　　)56. The newly wedded couple are going to buy some porcelains to decorate their home.

(　　)57. The company is upgrading their recreational room. Mary is shopping and making the decision.

(　　)58. Each office is required to prepare a first-aid kit, so Mary is doing the shopping.

(　　)59. Jane is shopping with her children and she wants to buy a scarf.

(　　)60. To diversify employees' leisure activities, the company wants to purchase some building blocks. So Zack is doing the shopping.

Section D (40%)

In this section, you will read 4 passages. After each passage, choose from A, B, and C the best answer for each question. (在本节中，你将读到4篇短文。从A、B、C三个选项中选出最佳答案。)

Passage A

The Guggenheim Museum attempts to help educators connect students with art. It offers programs for educators, including free arts curricula, professional development courses and workshops.

Visiting with your students: The museum offers a variety of ways to educators and their students to visit, from self-guided tours to a guided experience.

Guggenheim Museum Highlights	Perfect for first-time visitors, the Highlights Tour focuses on the museum's innovative architecture, history and permanent collection.
Special Exhibition	This tour offers an opportunity to engage in a lively, in-depth exploration of one of our special exhibitions. Learn about the artistic processes and movements behind some of the most revolutionary artists of the modern and contemporary age.
Custom Tour	Tours can be customized to accommodate a variety of interests, learning styles and subject matters. Our gallery educators can create a one-of-a-kind experience tailored to your group's needs.
Lecturer's Badge	Conduct a group tour of up to 20 people.

Arts curriculum online: The Guggenheim produces free curriculum materials on exhibitions for educators to use both during school visits and in the classroom. While the material focuses on recent exhibitions, a comprehensive range of lessons cover many works and artists in the museum's collection.

Learning Through Art: Learning Through Art sends experienced teaching artists into New York City public schools where they work with classroom teachers to develop and facilitate art projects into the school curriculum.

Education facilities: Housed in Sackler Center for Arts Education, the Guggenheim's education facilities include studio art and multimedia labs, a theater, an exhibition gallery, and a conference room.

(　　)61. Who are the museum's programs intended for?

　　　A. Students.　　　B. Parents.　　　C. Educators.　　　D. Artists.

( )62. Which tour can be designed based on your own interest?

    A. Custom Tour.   B. Lecturer's Badge.

    C. Special Exhibition.   D. Guggenheim Museum Highlights.

( )63. Which tour specializes in giving you an insight into revolutionary artists of modern and contemporary age?

    A. Custom Tour.   B. Lecturer's Badge.

    C. Special Exhibition.   D. Guggenheim Museum Highlights.

( )64. How do teaching artists help to make art projects into the school curriculum?

    A. By giving lessons online.   B. By working with teachers.

    C. By providing free materials.   D. By designing projects alone.

( )65. Where is Guggenheim Museum?

    A. In Billey Linein Center.   B. In Sackler Center.

    C. In Multimedia Labs.   D. At Guggenheim conference hall.

Passage B

Where Are the World's Best Beaches?

The American travel website company TripAdvisor publishes a list of the world's best beaches every year. Today, we are going to explore some of this year's best beaches in the world.

Baia do Sancho, Brazil

It's named as this year's best beach in the world. Its water is calm and clear. Its sand is fine and soft. But getting to Baia do Sancho is not so easy. It's on Fernando de Noronha, a volcanic island more than 300 kilometers off Brazil's coast. Travelers must take a plane or boat from major cities in northern Brazil to get there. And no more than 420 visitors can be on the island at one time.

Grace Bay, Turks and Caicos

While Baia do Sancho is difficult to get to, TripAdvisor's second-ranked beach couldn't be much easier for tourists to reach. This beach has impossibly clean and clear waters and pure white sand. Its calm waters make it extremely safe for swimming, snorkeling(浮潜), or simply floating. Once on land, many visitors enjoy walking barefoot for several kilometers on the soft, warm sand.

Eagle Beach, Aruba

To get to the third-best beach, we head south to the Dutch Caribbean island of Aruba. Like Grace Bay, Eagle Beach has clear, calm waters and soft white sand. It offers visitors a chance to try different water sports, including tubing and jet skiing. Eagle Beach may be best known, however, for its dramatic sunsets. On clear nights, the sky turns red, orange, and purple.

Playa Paraiso, Cuba

The fourth-best beach is Playa Paraiso, an island off Cuba's southern coast. It has a fun, <u>laid-back</u> restaurant for those who wish to eat, drink and do nothing all day. There is little else on the beach. And that is exactly what visitors like about it.

( )66. Which of the following best describes Baia do Sancho?

    A. It receives thousands of visitors daily.   B. It can only be visited by plane.

C. It is near Brazil's coast.　　　　　D. It is hard to reach.

(　　)67. How does Grace Bay attract tourists?

    A. By its colorful sand.　　　　　B. By its waters and sand.

    C. By its dangerous position.　　　　D. By its quiet environment for hiking.

(　　)68. Where can visitors go if they want to enjoy the beauty of the sinking sun?

    A. Baia do Sancho, Brazil.　　　　B. Grace Bay, Turks and Caicos.

    C. Eagle Beach, Aruba.　　　　　D. Playa Paraiso, Cuba.

(　　)69. What does the underlined word "laid-back" mean in the passage?

    A. Far away.　　B. Relaxed.　　C. Busy.　　D. Dusty.

(　　)70. What is TripAdvisor?

    A. A tourist agent.　　B. An online app.　　C. A famous magazine.　　D. A website company.

Passage C

NJSM Early Learning Programs

Created especially for preschool and kindergarten, our programs introduce science, history and art through creative play, stories and songs. Advance reservations are required.

Length: 45 minutes to one hour.

Cost: Varies according to program details.

Group Size: 15 to 20 students per workshop(研习班) session.

Reservations and Information: Call 609-292-1382 or e-mail *njsm.reservations@sos.nj.gov*.

NEW! Dino Motion

$2 per student

Young scientists launch their studies by looking into the world around them—beginning in their own backyard! Meet specimens(样本) from the museums' natural history collections along the way to learn how New Jersey's wildlife communicates through sound, body language, scent, and color. This interactive program features object-based learning as well as music, dance and imaginative play.

Paint Me a Story

$2 per student

Art and storytelling go hand in hand. Children explore the American Perspectives Gallery and discover the stories that paintings tell through color, themes and feelings. Children end the session in the studio using real art materials and techniques to paint their own unique story.

Stars and Shapes Forever

$3 per student

This two-part program will introduce young children to astronomy! Meet stars of all sizes and colors, model our solar system with creative play and create your own star to take home.

Discovery Den

For free

Visit our natural science play space, designed just for pre-kindergarten kids. Explore nature in New Jersey through touchable specimens, games, books, costumes and more! Maximum 15 students with adult supervision(监

督) are allowed at one time in this self-guided space.

( )71. What can kids learn from *NEW! Dino Motion*?

    A. The ways to build backyards.   B. The ways of using body language.

    C. The ways to make use of the outside world.   D. The ways of how wildlife communicates.

( )72. Which of the following programs can help kids learn astronomic knowledge?

    A. *NEW! Dino Motion*.   B. *Paint Me a Story*.

    C. *Stars and Shapes Forever*.   D. *Discovery Den*.

( )73. How can you sign up for *Discovery Den*?

    A. By making a call.   B. By signing up on-site.

    C. By writing a letter.   D. By visiting it yourself.

( )74. What should you do to join the four programs?

    A. Pay fees.   B. Reserve first.

    C. Join a workshop first.   D. Have adult companions.

( )75. Which program is the cheapest?

    A. *NEW! Dino Motion*.   B. *Paint Me a Story*.

    C. *Stars and Shapes Forever*.   D. *Discovery Den*.

Passage D

We need adult volunteer help in the mornings, while our student volunteers are otherwise occupied, to help us process donations and fill orders. With over 30,000 local children living in poverty, the need comes in great number! Winter is our busiest time of the year and we are busy with orders for warm clothes and school supplies. All those clothes should be sent out as soon as possible.

If you have a few morning hours to give, it would be very helpful, especially if you are able to bring a friend. It would also be helpful if you would forward this post to friends and family you think might be interested! They can have the chance to get in touch with us.

We need specific help at the aid agency:

Our Triage Department—Not exactly the perfect use of the word—for us triage means our first inspection of donations: sorting through thousands of donated items each week and deciding whether to keep them. If you must always find a place for everything, or if you think of yourself as a "picker" or "treasure hunter", then you re for us!

Our Order Department—Fill orders for gift packages—where volunteers take individual orders and "shop" at the aid agency, finding the best things for each child.

There is NO need to make an appointment to volunteer at the aid agency. In fact, we're a "drop-in" center for making a difference. We're open from Monday to Saturday and the best volunteer time for us is anytime between 9:00 a.m. and 2:00 p.m.

( )76. Why are more volunteers wanted during winter?

    A. People are poorer in winter.

    B. The agency only runs in winter.

    C. Poor children need help only in winter.

    D. A lot of warm clothes are needed in winter.

( )77. What would volunteers do at the aid agency?

    A. Choose proper items for the children in need.

    B. Get in touch with the poor children.

    C. Invite their friends to visit.

    D. Donate their warm clothes.

( )78. Who might be interested in the volunteer jobs at the aid agency?

    A. A person who loves shopping.

    B. A person who is busy in the morning.

    C. A person who is good at sorting out things.

    D. A person who wants to get some experience in writing posts.

( )79. What does the underlined word "shop" in Paragraph 5 refer to?

    A. Buy things.   B. Select things.   C. Enjoy things.   D. Destroy things.

( )80. When can we help at the aid agency?

    A. Anytime but you need to make an appointment beforehand.

    B. Anytime on Sundays.

    C. 4:00 p.m. on Sundays.

    D. 11:00 a.m. on Fridays.

听力文本

Section A

1. M: Hello, I want a cab.

   W: OK. What address is it?

   Q: What does the man want?

2. M: What's your job?

   W: I'm an accountant.

   Q: What's the woman's job?

3. M: Can you speak German?

   W: Yes, I can. I speak it very well.

   M: What else can you speak?

   W: Well, I know a little Italian.

   Q: Which language does the woman know a little?

4. M: Would you mind passing the salt, please?

   W: Certainly.

   Q: What did the man want?

5. W: May I take your order please?

   M: Yes, I'd like a Margarita pizza.

   Q: Where does the conversation take place?

6. W: I thought the department store was open late from Wednesday through Friday night.

   M: No, just Fridays.

   Q: On what night is the store open late?

7. W: What do you think of the lecture?

   M: I think it is very interesting. How about you?

   Q: What are the speakers talking about?

8. W: What are you going to do after graduation?

   M: I'm thinking about further my study abroad. How about you?

   Q: What is the relationship between the two speakers?

9. W: We are late. The play starts at 19:30.

   M: Take it easy. We still have 15 minutes.

   Q: What's the time now?

10. W: Are we ready to set off?

    M: Sorry, Mrs Lin. I can't find my passport.

    Q: What is missing?

Section B

Claire: Thank you for coming to see me, Michelle. I have your job application here. It looks very good. May I ask you some questions?

Michelle: Yes, of course, Mrs Jones.

Claire: Can you type, Michelle?

Michelle: Yes, I can. I can type sixty words per minute.

Claire: Oh, good. I need someone who can help me with my business correspondence, especially writing letters and reports.

Michelle: That's no problem. I can write business letters and reports. I have some examples here with me.

Claire: Thank you, Michelle. Hmm. These reports look excellent. Now I have a few overseas clients. Can you speak any languages?

Michelle: Yes, I can speak French quite well.

Claire: Oh, that's wonderful. Two of my new clients are from France. I can speak Spanish and Italian but not French! Now my last question is can you work two days a week on any two days and sometimes at the weekend?

Michelle: I can work any two days during the week. But I can't work at the weekend. I have a small child and I want to be at home at weekends.

Claire: I see. That's fine. Well, thank you for coming.

Section C

Interviewer: Good afternoon, Mr Lee. Thanks for coming today.

Mr Lee: I'm glad to be here.

Interviewer: A lot of listeners write and say they want to know more about important people in our community.

Would you mind answering a few questions about your daily life?

Mr Lee: Not at all.

Interviewer: Do you have an early start?

Mr Lee: Yes. I get up early, and read the newspaper. I always read the paper because it's very important for my work. I need to know all the business and finance news.

Interviewer: I see. When do you leave home?

Mr Lee: At about seven. I often go to work before eight, six days a week.

Interviewer: What do you do when you get to work?

Mr Lee: First I speak to my assistant, to discuss our work for the day. Sometimes I have to read reports. Sometimes I go to meetings. Sometimes I visit our branches. I'm always very busy.

Interviewer: Yes. Do you have any spare time?

Mr Lee: Not very much, I'm afraid. I'd like to spend more time with my family, but I often have important dinners with clients and other business people. Sometimes, I get a chance to have dinner at home.

Interviewer: Do you have any hobbies?

Mr Lee: Well, I like walking the dog. I always go for a walk after dinner with our dog, Rufus.

答案

1—5 CBCBB	6—10 ACBBB	11—15 BACBC	16—20 ADCEB
21—25 DAAAD	26—30 DDDCC	31—35 BDDBC	36—40 ACBAA
41—45 CEBDA	46—50 BCEAD	51—55 BDJLA	56—60 GHFCE
61—65 CACBB	66—70 DBCBD	71—75 DCABD	76—80 DACBD

试题（二）

本次考试包括听力和阅读两部分,共55道题目。请在1小时之内完成。

听力测试现在开始。

Part I   Listening 听力（20%）

Section A (10%)

In this section, you will hear 10 short sentences and questions. There are three pictures marked A, B, and C for each question. Choose the one that best matches the question. Each sentence and question will be read just once and you will have 15 seconds for each question.（在本节中,你将听到10个句子和相应的问题。每道题配有 A、B、C 三幅图片,选出与题目内容相符的一幅图片。每个句子和问题读一遍,每题你有15秒钟的作答时间。）

(   )1. Where might the woman work in the future?

I ♥ 上海

A.　北京 Beijing　　B.　　C. 广州

(　　)2. Where is the woman?

A.　　B.　　C.

(　　)3. What does the woman do?

A.　　B.　　C.

(　　)4. What's the woman's hobby?

A.　　B.　　C.

(　　)5. What does the woman prefer to do?

A.　　B.　　C.

(　　)6. How does Doris feel?

A.　　B.　　C.

(　　)7. What is the woman doing?

A.　　B.　　C.

(　　)8. Who is the woman talking to?

A.　　B.　　C.

(   )9. What was the woman doing last night?

A.

B.

C.

(   )10. What is the woman's job?

A.

B.

C.

Section B (5%)

In this section, you will hear a dialogue. After the dialogue, five questions will be asked. There are three choices marked A, B, and C for each question. Choose the one that best answers the question. The dialogue and questions will be read just once and you will have 15 seconds for each question.(在本节中,你将听到1段对话和5个相应的问题。每道题配有A、B、C三个选项,选出与题目内容相符合的一个答案。对话和每个问题读一遍,每题你有15秒钟的作答时间。)

(   )11. What does Jane do?

A. A waitress.　　　　B. A guide.　　　　C. A receptionist.

(   )12. What's the relationship between the two speakers?

A. Friends.　　　　B. Classmates.　　　　C. Colleagues.

(   )13. When will the man go to the restaurant?

A. Tonight.　　　　B. Tomorrow.　　　　C. Not yet decided.

(   )14. Which bus should the man take?

A. No. 503 Bus.　　　　B. No. 530 Bus.　　　　C. No. 533 Bus.

(   )15. Where is the restaurant?

A. Near the woman's apartment.

B. In front of the Grand Theatre.

C. In front of the Grand Theatre bus stop.

Section C (5%)

In this section, you will hear a dialogue. Fill in the blanks according to what you hear. The dialogue will be read just once. You will have one minute to complete the task. (在本节中,你将听到1段较长的对话。请根据对话内容填空。对话仅读1遍。你将有1分钟的作答时间。)

A. separate room	B. South Side	C. $80–$100
D. Chinese (student)	E. two	

```
                    The Host Family
Location: In the 16. _____.
Requirements for tenant: 17. _____.
Home background: With 18. _____ kids.
Facilities provided: 19. A _____.
Price: 20. _____ a week.
```

Part II   Reading 阅读(80%)

Section A (20%)

In this section, you will read 20 short dialogues or pictures. Choose from A, B, and C the choice that best completes the dialogue, sentence or answers the question.(在本节中,你将读到20个短对话或图片,从A、B、C三个选项中选出能够补全对话、句子或回答问题的最恰当的选项。)

(   )21. —He isn't a policeman, is he?

　　　　—_____. He works in a hospital.

　　　　A. Yes, he is　　　　　　B. No，he isn't　　　　　C. No，he is

(   )22. —Would you like to have another cup of coffee?

　　　　—_____.

　　　　A. Yes, I do　　　　　　B. No, thanks　　　　　C. Help yourself

(   )23. —You are not going out today, are you?

　　　　—_____. I want to go shopping.

　　　　A. Yes, I am not　　　　B. No, I'm not　　　　　C. Yes, I am

(   )24. —Is Jim in?

　　　　—Sorry, he's not at home.

　　　　—_____?

　　　　—Yes, please.

　　　　A. Do you want to see him　　B. What's the matter　　C. Can I take a message

(   )25. —Hello! 467893?

　　　　—Hello. Is that Tom?

　　　　—_____.

　　　　A. Yes, I am　　　　　　B. Yes, speaking　　　　　C. Yes, glad to meet you

(   )26. —It's an unlucky day! My bag has been stolen.

　　　　—_____

　　　　A. Really unlucky! I'm so sad.

　　　　B. No hurry! I can help you.

　　　　C. Bad luck! I'm sorry to hear that.

(   )27. —How beautiful your skirt is!

　　　　—_____.

A. I don't think so B. You are welcome C. Thank you

(   )28. —May I call you Johnson?

　　—_____.

A. Of course, if you like B. That's OK C. I've no idea

(   )29. —Must we leave now?

　　—_____. We still have two more hours.

A. Yes, we must B. No, we needn't C. No, we mustn't

(   )30. —Mr Brown is a hard-working man and he has achieved great success.

　　—_____.

A. So is Mr Green B. So has Mr Green C. It's the same with Mr Green

(   )31. —Do you have Huawei P30 mobiles?

　　—_____. You may come next week.

A. Sorry, they have been sold out B. Yes, I do C. No, I haven't

(   )32. —Jenny, you have got the first prize in the competition. Congratulations!

　　—_____.

A. That's my good luck B. Oh, it's nothing C. Thank you

(   )33. —If you have any trouble, be sure to call me.

　　—_____.

A. I will. Thank you very much B. I'm glad to hear that C. I have no trouble

(   )34. —Would you like to go to the ballet next Friday? I've got two tickets.

　　—_____.

A. I'll think about it B. No, I'm busy now C. Oh, that sounds like fun

(   )35. —Excuse me. Is it my turn now? I have been waiting for some time and I am wondering...

　　—_____. The doctor is busy.

A. No, you aren't B. Yes, it's your turn C. I'm sorry

(   )36. —How beautiful! How long have you had it?

　　—_____.

A. Two weeks ago B. Only two weeks C. Tonight

(   )37. —Be quiet, please. Can I remind you what you should do?

　　—_____.

A. Go ahead, please B. Yes, you can C. No, you can't

(   )38. —Lisa, why do you want to give up your present job?

　　—_____.

A. I don't know B. It's so exciting C. I'd like to try something different

(   )39. —Would you like to see a menu?

　　—_____. I already know what to order.

A. Yes, please B. No, thanks C. Give me a second

(   )40. —You don't feel very well, do you? You look pale. Have you got a cold?

　　—_____. Maybe the seafood doesn't agree with me.

A. Yes, I have	B. No, I haven't	C. Oh, no, but my stomach aches

Section B (10%)

In this section, you will read 2 dialogues. For each blank, choose from A, B, C, D, and E the expression that best completes the dialogue. （在本节中，你将读到 2 段对话。从 A、B、C、D、E 五个选项中选出能够补全对话的最恰当的选项。）

Dialogue 1

A. fit in	B. in the district	C. coming for
D. welcome party	E. the middle of	

A: Linda, do you know when the visitors from India are coming?

B: They had three choices: the end of March, _____41_____ April and the beginning of May, and they chose the earliest one.

A: Right. And how many are coming? Did you say about 8?

B: Yes, they said 8 at first, but changed to 6 this morning.

A: Good, we have 5 weeks to prepare. Here are my suggestions. On the first day, we can hold a _____42_____, then they can visit the schools _____43_____ on the second and third days.

B: We've got to remember this group wants to look at how the Internet is being used in classroom. That's what they are _____44_____.

A: Exactly, so I want to ask Mr. Todd to give them a talk on this in the afternoon of the third day.

B: That will _____45_____ very nicely.

Dialogue 2

A. sales volume	B. current job	C. within the week
D. working conditions	E. past work achievements	

A: Good morning, madam. I'm Daniel. I'm looking for the position of manager.

B: Sit down, please. How did you learn about our company?

A: I got to know your company through such famous brands as LUX, LITOS and WALLS. Your products impressed me deeply.

B: Well, please tell me something about your _____46_____.

A: All right, madam. When working for my previous company, I succeeded in raising the yearly _____47_____ by 25%.

B: Oh, that is quite an achievement. Why have you decided to change jobs?

A: I hope to change because I am looking a more challenging position. There are no more opportunities for me to grow in my _____48_____.

B: OK, I understand. But why have you made the choice to work for us?

A: I have carefully studied the information about your company on the Internet and I have checked your company's homepage. The _____49_____ are so excellent here. I sincerely hope to be a member of your company.

B: That's fine. Thanks for coming to see us. I will let you know about the job _____50_____ .

Section C (10%)

The following chart shows a list of departments in a hotel. Decide which department each person works in.(下面是某酒店的部门列表。请根据描述将每个人与其所在的部门名称相匹配。)

A. Housekeeping Department	B. Front Desk Department
C. Accounting Department	D. Sales Department
E. Maintenance Department	F. Catering Department
G. Kitchen Department	H. Concierge Department
I. Executive Team	J. Public Relations Department

(　　)51. Tim offers a great variety of scrumptious dishes to keep hungry customers happy.

(　　)52. Kim provides the hotel with relevant financial data and forecasts which are used for daily decision making to ensure we are thriving and keeping the books up to date.

(　　)53. Henry is one of the members to ensure the smooth running of hotel operations. He is responsible for the management of his own department and finds ways to continuously improve business profitability and guest experience.

(　　)54. Sam is in charge of negotiating and prospecting large business and leisure groups, tour operators and individual travellers.

(　　)55. Teressa's work involves increasing exposure for the hotel through various advertising opportunities both in print and on the Web. She knows a lot of people in the media circle.

(　　)56. Nick performs a wide range of essential tasks to help ensure the smooth operation of equipment and facilities.

(　　)57. Anna is in charge of almost every detail of your stay from the fluffy pillows and sheets in your guest rooms to the replenishment of your bathroom amenities.

(　　)58. Terry is constantly providing guests various information, such as the travel routes, recommendations of tours, attractions, and short cuts around the town.

(　　)59. Rose is expected to have good communication skills, conduct multi tasks and work with passion for she has direct contact with guests.

(　　)60. Mark works in the department that is well positioned to provide food and refreshments for weddings, other celebratory events, conferences, etc.

Section D (40%)

In this section, you will read 4 passages. After each passage, choose from A, B, and C the best answer for each question.(在本节中,你将读到4篇短文。从A、B、C三个选项中选出最佳答案。)

Passage A

Do you know there is a job called party planner? This kind of job is so popular in western countries that people can not only have high pay, but also use their creativity to plan parties.

As a party planner, you will be hired to create some of the most memorable moments of people's lives and give people the chance to communicate, celebrate and have fun.

Few careers offer so many benefits. As a party planner, you will have an interesting and fun job. The most attractive part is when you start your own planning business, you can enjoy the freedom of being your own boss.

You can organize all types of parties as a party planner or choose certain types you enjoy most such as:

- Anniversary party
- Birthday party
- Children's party
- Dinner party
- Engagement party
- Family reunions
- Graduation party
- Holiday party
- Open house party
- Theme party
- And more!

A party planner will handle every detail of the party, or just one aspect. If you have the desire, you can become a party planner. No special education or experience is necessary to break into this career.

( )61. Why does "party planner" become a popular job in the West?

    A. Get high pay.   B. Use creativity to plan parties.   C. Both A and B.

( )62. What can a party planner create for others?

    A. Nice food.   B. Interesting games.   C. Memorable moments.

( )63. What's the biggest benefit of being a party planner?

    A. It's interesting and fun.

    B. Have the freedom to be your own boss.

    C. Give people the chance to communicate, celebrate and have fun.

( )64. What types of parties can a party planner organize?

    A. All types.   B. Some certain types.   C. Both A and B.

( )65. If someone wants to be a party member, what does he need to have?

    A. Desire.   B. Special education.   C. Experience.

Passage B

August 13th, 2014

Dear sir,

I am very happy to apply for the position of secretary, which you advertised in *China Daily* of August the 11th, 2014.

I have been working as a secretary at a college office. Because I am the only secretary in the office, it is necessary for me to work quickly and efficiently and to be flexible in my daily work. Professors value my work and my ability to meet their needs.

Although I am happy now, I feel that my promotion is limited here. And I would like to have a more challenging job. Therefore I enrolled in a program to expand my knowledge of international business affairs. Now both my Chinese and English have been improved, and I am ready to begin working as a bilingual secretary in an international company like yours. And I believe I can be a great help to your firm.

The enclosed resume gives further details of my qualifications, and I would appreciate it if you should give me an opportunity to have an interview. I am looking forward to receiving your call at 32786543.

Thank you very much for your consideration.

Faithfully yours,

Mary Lee

(　　)66. Where does the writer get the job information?

　　A. From magazines.　　　　　B. From the Internet.　　　　C. From the newspaper.

(　　)67. The writer wants to change her job because _____.

　　A. she has difficulty handling her daily work efficiently

　　B. she can hardly get a chance to be promoted

　　C. she finds her present job too challenging

(　　)68. A bilingual secretary differs from other secretaries in that she can _____.

　　A. do the job efficiently

　　B. write official documents

　　C. speak two languages

(　　)69. By sending this letter, the writer expected to _____.

　　A. draw the attention of the company

　　B. get an opportunity for an interview

　　C. apply for a suitable position in *China Daily*

(　　)70. What qualifications does the writer have?

　　A. The knowledge of international business affairs.

　　B. Computer skills.

　　C. Communication skills.

Passage C

The Seine River Cruise By Night		
Enjoy your wonderful dinner on the ferry and		
See the fantastic city lights		
Time: 7:00 p.m. —10:00 p.m. daily		
Price:	with dinner	without dinner
Adult:	$130	$90
Children under 12:	$80	$50
Start/Stop: La Marina Port de Solférino — Quai Anatole France		
Ticket Office: Star Company (23 Marina Road)		

(　　)71. The cruise will begin _____.

A. at seven in the morning   B. at seven in the evening   C. at ten in the morning

(　　)72. The cruise will take _____.

A. 30 minutes   B. 3 minutes   C. 3 hours

(　　)73. Mr King can see _____ during the cruise.

A. bridges   B. buildings   C. fantastic city lights

(　　)74. People can buy tickets _____.

A. at 23 Marina Road   B. La Marina Port de Solferino   C. Quai Anatole France

(　　)75. Helen wants to have dinner on the ferry with her son, 14, and her daughter, 10, they should pay _____.

A. $340   B. $290   C. $270

Passage D

No one wants to look silly or do the wrong things at a new job. It is important to make the right impression from the very first day because you will face new people. It may be difficult to know what to do. Here are five tips to help you make it through the first day at a new job:

1. First impressions can last forever. Make sure you make a good one. Before your first day, find out if your new job has a dress code rule about what you can wear to work. If so, be sure to follow it and always be neat and clean.

2. Get to work on time. Give yourself an extra 15 minutes to make sure you arrive on time.

3. Pay attention to introductions. One of the first things that your supervisor may do is to introduce you to the co-workers. These co-workers will be important to you. They are the ones who will answer the questions when the boss is not around.

4. Ask plenty of questions. Make sure that your supervisor has told you what is expected of you. If he or she has not told you your duties, ask for a list and set daily and weekly goals for yourself.

5. Never be the first one to leave. Observe what your co-workers do around quitting time. It does not look good for you to be eager to leave.

(　　)76. Before you arrive at work, you should _____.

A. dress in a right way   B. introduce yourself   C. know your duties

(　　)77. According to the passage, which of the following statements is TRUE?

A. You should be the first one to arrive at work.

B. You should ask your co-workers for your duties.

C. You should not be eager to go back home.

(　　)78. According to the passage, your supervisor is most likely your _____.

A. visitor   B. workmate   C. leader

(　　)79. The writer thinks that a new job is _____ to people.

A. a duty   B. a challenge   C. an offer

(　　)80. What is the best title for this passage?

A. Getting a new job   B. Tips on how to work   C. The first-day work

听力文本

Section A

1. W: The Pudong area is developing so fast. I really want to work here after my graduation.

   Q: Where might the woman work in the future?

2. W: Wow, your apartment is such a mess.

   Q: Where is the woman?

3. W: The New Year is coming. The final examination is approaching as well.

   Q: What does the woman do?

4. W: I like climbing. Are you fond of it?

   Q: What's the woman's hobby?

5. W: I'd rather stay at home, because singing is not my cup of tea.

   Q: What does the woman prefer to do?

6. W: Hi, Doris. You look a little bit down. What's the matter?

   Q: How does Doris feel?

7. W: I'm here to apply for the job of director that your company posted yesterday. Is it still available?

   Q: What is the woman doing?

8. W: I'm afraid you've made a mistake. This isn't what I ordered.

   Q: Who is the woman talking to?

9: W: I stayed up all night to finish my paper.

   Q: What was the woman doing last night?

10. W: Hi, Customer Service Desk. What can I do for you today, sir?

    Q: What is the woman's job?

Section B

M: How is your job doing, Jane?

W: Great! I'm enjoying it a lot. The restaurant is really busy, and the tips are good.

M: I should come and have dinner sometime.

W: Yes, why don't you? I will always welcome an old classmate. You will enjoy our food. I think it's best.

M: OK. I will go tomorrow.

W: Do you know how to get there?

M: Not really.

W: Well, it's not far from your apartment. Take No. 503 Bus and get off at the Grand Theatre Station. Then you can find it just right in front of the bus stop.

Section C

Adviser: Good morning, we have verified your information. Do you have any special requirements for the host family?

Student: Yeah, I hope to find a host family near my college. That will be convenient for my study.

Adviser: That's reasonable. Well, where is your college?

Student: It's in the South Side.

Adviser: OK. Let me see. Oh, there are three host families, and one of them specifies that they need a Chinese student.

Student: That's perfect. Er, are there any kids in the family?

Adviser: Yes, there are two children, a seven-year-old girl and a five-year-old boy.

Student: Well, will they offer me a separate room?

Adviser: Yes, you can have a separate room, but you will be charged 80—100 dollars a week. Could you afford it?

Student: That sounds good. Can you help me contact this family?

Adviser: OK, we will inform you at once if we get any responses.

答案

1—5 BACBC	6—10 BAACA	11—15 ABBAC	16—20 BDEAC
21—25 BBCCB	26—30 CCABC	31—35 ACACC	36—40 BACBC
41—45 EDBCA	46—50 EABDC	51—55 GCIDJ	56—60 EAHBF
61—65 CCBCA	66—70 CBCBA	71—75 BCCAA	76—80 ACCBC

试题（三）

Part I   Listening 听力（20%）

Section A (10%)

In this section, you will hear 10 short dialogues and questions. There are three pictures marked A, B, and C for each question. Choose the one that best matches the question. Each dialogue and question will be read just once and you will have 15 seconds for each question.（在本节中，你将听到10个短对话和相应的问题。每道题配有A、B、C三幅图片，选出与题目内容相符合的一幅图片。每个对话和问题读一遍，每题你有15秒钟的作答时间。）

(   )1. Where does this conversation most likely take place?

 A.    B.    C.

(   )2. Why is Lisa late for the party?

 A.    B.    C.

( )3. What is the relationship between the speakers?

 A.　　 B.　　 C.

( )4. What will the man do tomorrow?

 A.　　 B.　　 C.

( )5. Which sign should the man pay attention to?

 A.　　 B.　　 C.

( )6. Where does this conversation most likely take place?

 A.　　 B.　　 C.

( )7. What is the woman's job?

 A.　　 B.　　 C.

( )8. What does the woman want to do?

 A.　　 B.　　 C.

( )9. Why does the woman want to buy a gift for her boyfriend?

 A.　　 B.　　 C.

( )10. Where did the woman take her photos?

 A.　　 B.　　 C.

Section B (5%)

In this section, you will hear a dialogue. After the dialogue, five questions will be asked. There are three choices marked A, B, and C for each question. Choose the one that best answers the question. The dialogue and questions will be read just once and you will have 15 seconds for each question.(在本节中,你将听到1段对话和5个相应的问题。每道题配有A、B、C三个选项,选出与题目内容相符合的一个答案。对话和每个问题读一遍,每题有15秒钟的作答时间。)

(   )11. What is the relationship between the woman and the man?

      A. Colleagues.   B. Siblings.   C. A couple.

(   )12. What is the woman reading?

      A. A novel.   B. Newspapers.   C. Ads.

(   )13. What course is the woman particularly looking for?

      A. Literature.   B. Sports.   C. Painting.

(   )14. What is their son doing on Thursday evenings?

      A. Having English lessons.   B. Having Gobang classes.   C. Having Piano classes.

(   )15. What course do they consider to consult?

      A. Badminton on Thursdays.   B. Badminton on Tuesdays.   C. Basketball on Tuesdays.

Section C (5%)

In this section, you will hear a dialogue. After the dialogue, arrange the following activities in the correct order.(在本节中,你将听到1段对话。根据对话中的内容将下列活动排序。)

A. Current medication	B. Address	C. Previous operations
D. Details of illnesses	E. Allergic reaction	

16. _____   17. _____   18. _____   19. _____   20. _____

Part Ⅱ　Reading 阅读(80%)

Section A (20%)

In this section, you will read 20 short dialogues or pictures. Choose from A, B, and C the choice that best completes the dialogue, sentence or answers the question. (在本节中,你将读到20个短对话或图片,从A、B、C三个选项中选出能够补全对话、句子或回答问题的最恰当的选项。)

(   )21. —Mark, please don't play basketball on the road. It's very dangerous.

      —_____. I am going home at once.

      A. Have a great time   B. Sorry, I won't do that again   C. I'd like to

(   )22. —China beat Australia 1:0 at the 17th Women's Football Asian Cup last night.

      —Really? _____.

      A. That's a pity   B. Don't mention it   C. I'm glad to hear that

(   )23. —Would you like me to show you the way?

      —_____.

A. Yes, you would   B. It's right   C. That's very kind of you

( )24. —It's really nice of you to help me!

—_____

A. My pleasure.   B. Don't say that.   C. Is that so?

( )25. —Shall we see the movie today or tomorrow?

—_____. It's all the same to me.

A. I hope so   B. I'm sure   C. It's up to you

( )26. How could you get in touch with a librarian?

Have a Question?
A librarian is only
a click away.

Chat   Email   Meet

Ask a Librarian
http://library.uvm.edu/guides/ask

A. Send an email.   B. Make a phone call.   C. Go to the office.

( )27. Here's the timetable of the National Visa Center. You can hand in your application forms on _____.

BUSINESS HOURS	A.M.	P.M.
MONDAY	8:00	5:30
TUESDAY	8:00	5:30
WEDNESDAY	8:00	5:30
THURSDAY	8:00	5:30
FRIDAY	8:00	5:30
SATURDAY	9:00	12:30
SUNDAY	CLOSED	

A. Tuesday, 7:00 a.m.   B. Saturday, 5:00 p.m.   C. Thursday, 9:00 a.m.

( )28. Which statement about this poster is probably TRUE?

GOOD DAY BEGINS WITH COFFEE

SERVED HERE.   HAVE A CUP!

A. You may see this sign outside a restaurant.

B. Coffee is one of the cheapest ways to be happy.

C. People are addicted to coffee.

( )29. The signs on the packing box show that _____.

A. there is a glass, two arrows and an umbrella in the box

B. we should be very careful when delivering this box

C. the product inside the box might be a pair of shoes

( )30. To create a Facebook account, you need to provide all the information EXCEPT _____.

A. Postcode   B. Birthday   C. Family name

( )31. —Thank you very much for giving me some advice on how to deal with stress.

　—_____.

A. That's true   B. Don't mention it   C. OK, I'll try

( )32. —Excuse me. May I use your eraser, please?

　—Sure. _____

A. Watch out!   B. Well done!   C. Go ahead.

( )33. —I hope you don't mind my opening the window.

　—_____. It's much too hot in here.

A. Certainly   B. Of course not   C. All right

( )34. —Mike hurt his arm the day before yesterday. Now he's in hospital.

　—_____.

A. I'm sorry to hear that   B. That's all right   C. I hope you'll feel better soon

(   )35. —Hello, this is Tina speaking. Is that Sam?

—Sorry, he isn't here at this moment. _____?

A. Can I take a message   B. What are you saying to Tina   C. May I speak to Sam

(   )36. During which period could Liu Qianxia stay in Myanmar according to her visa?

A. From 13 Jan. 2012 to 12 Apr. 2012.

B. From 13 Jan. 2012 to 23 Jan. 2012.

C. From 1 Mar. 2012 to 12 Apr. 2012.

(   )37. Here's the map of a shopping center. You can't _____ there.

A. purchase some medicine   B. watch the latest movie   C. do physical exercises

(   )38. Which statement about this poster is probably TRUE?

A. You may see this poster inside a hospital.

B. The poster calls on people to protect the earth.

C. The designer of this poster is a radical environmentalist.

(   )39. According to the sign, David could do all of the followings EXCEPT _____.

A. drive at a speed of 60 km/h   B. hit a kangaroo   C. drive before the sunset

40. Jane just arrives in Lishe Airport and is going to collect her luggage. She should _____.

A. go upstairs   B. go downstairs   C. turn right

Section B (10%)

In this section, you will read 2 dialogues. For each blank, choose from A, B, C, D, and E the expression that best completes the dialogue.(在本节中,你将读到2段对话。从A、B、C、D、E五个选项中选出能够补全对话的最恰当的选项。)

Dialogue 1

A. with luggage	B. reservation form	C. pick it up
D. availability	E. if it's possible	

A: Good morning, Alien Car Hire. How can I help you?

B: I'm calling to see _____41_____ to hire a car for three days next weekend.

A: What size of the car are you hoping to rent?

B: Well, something big enough for a family of four _____42_____.

A: That would be a medium family car. Let's see... Yes, that shouldn't be a problem—there's plenty of _____43_____.

B: Great! What's the earliest time for us to _____44_____?

A: Our office opens at 8 am.

B: Oh, not that early. I expect that about a quarter to nine would suit us.

A: Ok, I'll write it down in your _____45_____.

Dialogue 2

> A. make up   B. order number   C. graduation ceremony
>
> D. online shop   E. due to

A: Good morning, ABC company. How can I help you?

B: I bought a pair of shoes from your _____46_____ 10 days ago but I haven't received it yet. Can you check it for me?

A: Sure. Could you give me your _____47_____, please?

B: It's 01234.

A: Let me see... Yeah, I find it. It has just been sent out.

B: How long will it take on the way?

A: Normally it will arrive in 5 days, but _____48_____ Double 11, it's hard to say...

B: Oh no! I planned to wear it on my _____49_____ the day after.

A: Sorry for the inconvenience caused to you. We'll send you a coupon later to _____50_____ for it.

Section C (10%)

The following list is about various departments of a hotel. Please match the department that the person needs to contact. (下面列表里包含酒店各个部门。请根据下面的情况匹配相关人员需要与之联系的部门。)

A. Public Relation Department	F. Food and Beverage Department
B. Finance Department	G. Engineering Department
C. Front Office Department	H. Recreation and Entertainment Department
D. Sales & Marketing Division	I. Human Resources Department
E. Reservation Department	J. Security Department

(   )51. Lisa is an artist agent for a popular star—Michael Bieber. She arranges his schedule, business and performance plans. Now she needs to make sure his safety when arriving the hotel in Nanjing.

(   )52. Peter is graduated from Cornell University this year, majoring in hospitality management. He has sent his resume to some of his dream hotels and is waiting for a job interview.

(   )53. The computers in front desk all collapsed down. Sophie needs some help to fix the problem, otherwise there will be a long line of customers.

(   )54. Recently, the issue of insanitation has been uncovered in social media and has been fiercely discussed. Jenny is reflecting her misconduct as CEO while she also finds Jerry from _____ to solace the storm.

( )55. Michael needs to change the entrees and main course of his wedding dinner.

( )56. Jack wants to check in before 10 am since he has a little jet-lag after such a long flight.

( )57. Alex insists to give a 25% off discount as a benefit for early booking in Spring Promotion to attract more customers.

( )58. Andy wants to know what activities he can do in the hotel when he statys there. For instance, can he play golf or take a sunbath on the beach?

( )59. Mary has been very busy calculating and summing up the revenue of last quarter in the financial report. She has been working overtime for almost 2 weeks.

( )60. Joe and his friends planned to have a vacation next week for 5 days. The time they will stay is a busy season and many rooms are occupied very early. Joe needs to book a room immediately.

Section D (40%)

In this section, you will read 4 passages. After each passage, choose from A, B, and C the best answer for each question. (在本节中，你将读到4篇短文。从A、B、C三个选项中选出最佳答案。)

Passage A

> To: Mark Jacob@yahoo.com
>
> Dearest Mark Jacob,
>
> Hi, I am writing this email to thank you for the birthday wishes and love that you sent to me through the wonderful birthday gift. I am filled with joy knowing that you care about my likes and took effort to find the perfect birthday gift for me. The portable music player is exactly the one which I wanted, and I have no words to express my feelings on receiving it.
>
> I have been telling my parents for months to get me a music player which I could carry easily with me, but they seemed to delay getting it for me each time. So this is why this gift is all the more special for me. Though you driving down here on my birthday would have made me happier, I wish to thank you once again for all the love.
>
> Love
>
> Fred Flintoff

( )61. Fred wrote this email mainly to _____.

A. ask for a birthday present

B. thank Mark for coming to his birthday party

C. thank Mark for buying him a birthday present

( )62. The relationship between Fred and Mark is probably _____.

A. classmates   B. colleagues   C. parents and children

( )63. Why is Fred so excited about the gift?

A. Because his parents bought it for him.

B. Because he has been dreaming of it for a long time.

C. Because the gift is of high quality.

( )64. It can be inferred from the passage that Mark chose the perfect gift by _____.

A. taking Fred's preference into consideration

B. asking Fred's parents

C. asking Fred directly

(   )65. We can learn from the passage that _____.

A. parents must buy a birthday gift for their children

B. buying your friend a gift is much more important than attending his birthday party

C. the best gift is the one that meets the needs

Passage B

> **Teachers Wanted**
>
> • Number: 10
>
> • Age: under 40
>
> • Certificate in TCSL (Teaching Chinese as A Second Language)
>
>   At least 2 years of teaching experience
>
>   Able to work 20 hours from Monday to Friday, and 8 hours at weekends
>
>   Proficient in French/ Spanish/ Italian/ German
>
> • Salary: 200,000 RMB per year
>
> • Base: Europe
>
> • Interview:
>
>   Room 101, Rainbow Building, Renmin Plaza
>
>   Timetable in individual notice. Keep your mobile phone on.
>
> • Application form before 15 January 2020
>
> • Any question please contact:
>
>   Tel: (010)-99996666
>
>   Email: Tcsl-bj@163.com
>
> TCSL Beijing
>
> 12 December 2019

(   )66. What position is wanted by TCSL Beijing?

A. French teachers.   B. English teachers.   C. Chinese teachers.

(   )67. Which is the qualification mentioned in the job advertisement?

A. Certificate in TCSL.   B. 5 years' teaching experience.   C. Speak fluent English.

(   )68. Where can the applicant attend the interview?

A. TCSL Beijing.

B. Europe.

C. Room 101, Rainbow Building, Renmin Plaza.

(   )69. How much can a teacher earn per month?

A. 200,000 RMB.   B. More than 15,000 RMB.   C. Less than 16,000 RMB.

( )70. When should applicants send the application form?

    A. After 15 January 2020.   B. Before 12 December 2019.   C. Before 15 January 2020.

Passage C

Just a short stroll away from the Shanghai Disneyland, your vacation fun continues at Toy Story Hotel, a place inspired by the amusing toys. The story-themed room with playful touches all around; Say hello to Woody and Jessie and take pictures with them just like run into your old friends; Here, you will be endued with vitality to enjoy the endless fun and you will smile as genuinely from heart as a kid.

What Makes This Resort Hotel Unique

A Place Inspired by the Amusing Toys

Experience a vacation like no other — immersed in the fun-filled world of *Toy Story*. Read More

Enjoy the Various Fun with Your Kids

Your kids can have a break anytime during your park visit. Read More

Reserve Disney Fastpass in Advance

Hotel Guests can reserve Disney Fastpass in advance in two different ways. Read More

Toy Story Hotel

Searching for Room Type and Price

Map

Hotel Address

Toy Story Hotel No.360 West Shendi Rd. Pudong New District, Shanghai, 201205, The People's Republic of China
+86-21-2099-8003

Complimentary self-parking available
Get Directions

( )71. Who will search information on this webpage?

    A. Hotel staff.   B. Disneyland staff.   C. Hotel guests.

( )72. What can you experience in the hotel?

    A. Take pictures with cartoon characters.

    B. Get free toys as souvenirs.

    C. Enter Disneyland without buying tickets.

( )73. If you want to know how much it will cost for one night, you should click "_____".

    A. A Place Inspired by the Amusing Toys

    B. Searching for Room Type and Price

    C. Get Directions

( )74. Which of the statements is TRUE?

    A. Kids will enjoy their stay in this hotel.

    B. Parking fee is quite cheap.

    C. Guests can get Fastpass whenever they want.

( )75. We can learn from the passage that this hotel _____.

    A. is far away from Disneyland   B. has story-themed rooms   C. is the best choice for visitors

Passage D

    It is no secret that many famous people, including Napoleon, Catherine the Great, and even the Queen of

England, loved silk clothes. In the thirteenth century, Marco Polo traveled the Silk Road and brought silk to Venice. You can be sure that Italians valued this precious material greatly. Some of the designs added into their clothing were copies of paintings by Leonardo da Vinci.

Today, there are no world-class dress designers who have not used Italian cloth materials made of Chinese silk. A famous poet has said, "What diamonds do for the hand, silk does for the body." Silk has a comfortable and expensive quality. Silk dresses and suits certainly add beauty and style to one's clothes collection. You want to be considered as successful, fashionable and have a good taste in clothes, don't you? Come and buy a silk dress or shirt today!

( )76. Who introduced silk to Europe?

    A. Napoleon.   B. Marco Polo.   C. Leonardo da Vinci.

( )77. Why is silk so popular?

    A. It's affordable for the poor.

    B. It's the best material for clothes.

    C. It feels comfortable and is of good quality.

( )78. What does the underlined sentence (para. 2) imply?

    A. Silk makes a person more beautiful and attractive.

    B. Silk is as expensive as diamonds.

    C. There's no difference between silk and diamonds.

( )79. Which of the statements is TRUE?

    A. You could buy a piece of silk in 1280 in Italy.

    B. Italians dislike silk clothes due to the high price.

    C. No one could succeed without silk clothes.

( )80. We can learn from the passage that silk _____.

    A. is considered as a cheap material for clothing

    B. can bring good fortune to its owner

    C. is a symbol of fashion and good taste

听力文本

Section A

1. M: May I have your passport, please?

    B: Sure, here you are.

    Q: Where does this conversation most likely take place?

2. W: Jimmy is on the way, but Lisa will be late for 30 minutes due to the traffic jam.

    M: Oh, I don't believe her. Jack says she got up too late.

    Q: Why is Lisa late for the party?

3. W: What do you think of this necklace?

    M: Wow, it's dazzling! My wife will definitely like it.

Q: What is the relationship between the speakers?

4. W: Shall we go hiking tomorrow?

   M: I'd like to, but I need to write a report, and prepare for the presentation next week.

   Q: What will the man do tomorrow?

5. W: You can't eat hamburgers in the library!

   M: I'm terribly sorry. I didn't see the sign.

   Q: Which sign should the man pay attention to?

6. M: There's a hole on the scarf. I'd like to return it.

   W: Sure. May I have your receipt?

   Q: Where does this conversation most likely take place?

7. W: What would you like to order, sir?

   M: A moment please. I haven't decided yet.

   Q: What is the woman's job?

8. M: Do you want to be an engineer like your father?

   W: No. My mum wants me to work in the hospital, but I prefer staying with kids.

   Q: What does the woman want to do?

9. W: I want to choose a birthday gift for my boyfriend.

   M: How about this watch?

   Q: Why does the woman want to buy a gift for her boyfriend?

10. M: The photos you posted online are amazing!

    W: Thanks! I love them, too. Paris is definitely the best place for wedding.

    Q: Where did the woman take her photos?

Section B

M: Honey, what are you doing?

W: I'm looking at some physical training ads for kids.

M: Why doing this?

W: The doctor said our boy's BMI score falls beyond the normal standard, which means he is a little bit fat. She suggested us to offer him more exercises.

M: OK, I get it. So any sports you like?

W: I think badminton is quite eye catchy. Swimming is not bad. Playing basketball is also within my consideration, because the basketball court may be the easiest sport field for boys to find at school.

M: No, no, no. It's too much for a just 5-year-old kid. Roy has already had painting classes on Wednesday evenings, English lessons on Thursday evenings, Gobang and piano classes on Friday and Saturday evenings. Oh, I almost forgot Lego architect training on Sunday mornings. I know our son needs physical exercises, but not more than one. Otherwise, it's off limit.

W: No worry. I'm just thinking about those options instead of doing all of them. We need focus and concentration, which is actually more reasonable and effective. So how about badminton on Tuesday afternoons?

M: We can contact those course consultants and have some ideas about the training time and intensity first.

W: Good advice. I'll make the phone call.

Section C (5%)

As a foreigner, if you want to see a doctor, you need to register first. Fill in the medical history form and give details of any illnesses you have had. You also need to write down if you've got any allergies. Besides, we need to know if you've had any operations before. Next, you have to give full details of current medication you may be on. Last of all, fill in this register card—this is for your personal details, your full name, address, and telephone numbers.

答案

1—5 ABBBC	6—10 ACABB	11—15 CCBAB	16—20 DECAB
21—25 BCCAC	26—30 ACABA	31—35 BCBAA	36—40 BCBBB
41—45 EADCB	46—50 DBECA	51—55 JIGAF	56—60 CDHBE
61—65 CABAC	66—70 CACBC	71—75 CABAB	76—80 BCAAC

第二节 环节二 主题产品营销

一、商贸

（一）模拟（一）

Amid the surging tide of garbage sorting/waste classification, people's awareness towards environmental protection is on the rise. Suppose you are a civil servant working in the bureau of ecology and environment. Design a product that can instruct people, especially senior citizens to properly sort different waste into the right bins or largely enhance the efficiency of garbage sorting.

You can choose any of your products you think appropriate. But the products must be commercially available. You will have two minutes to deliver your speech.

（二）模拟（二）

Suppose you are a marketing manager responsible for searching the most lucrative/best-selling products at the turn of winter. Choose one of the products that can dramatically improve the life quality of people during chilly seasons and give a presentation to promote it.

You can choose any of your products you think appropriate. But the products must be commercially available. You will have two minutes to deliver your speech.

二、旅游

（一）模拟（一）

Suppose you are the tour guide of overseas students who come to China for the first time. Design a one-day tour plan for the group and introduce to your target customer the highlights and significance of the trip.

You can choose any scenic spots/tourist attractions/places of interest in China. However, your plan must be practical and advertise the remarkable achievement made by PRC on the occasion of its 70th anniversary. You will have two minutes to deliver your presentation.

（二）模拟（二）

Suppose you are the marketing/planning director of a travel agency which conduct business both home and abroad. Design a two-day autumn outing for senior-high school students coming from Ireland and introduce to your target customer the highlights and significance of the trip.

You can choose any scenic spots/tourist attractions/places of interest in China. However, your plan must be feasible and related to the theme of the belt-and-road initiative. You will have two minutes to deliver your presentation.

（三）模拟（三）

Background:

A family from Shanghai plan to spend a weekend in the countryside in Ningbo in May. They want to taste some traditional local food and seek for an opportunity to contact with nature. They think it would be best if they could experience farm-based activities (Agritainment). Since they have a little kid at the age of 4, they are inclined to have the trip in the family-oriented style.

Your task: Plan a day-trip in one of counties in Ningbo, such as Fenghua, Xiangshan, etc. Please try to meet all the customers' requriments

Constant A: Introduce your trip plan to your customers within 3 minutes

Constant B: Answer 2−3 questions

Detailed mission:

• Discussion about your tourism product, including detailed tourism attractions, itinerary, your core conception of your service and so on.

• One PowerPoint covering the information you want to show.

• A well-prepard introduction. Don't forget to introduce your position.

第五章　补充

第一节　词汇训练

平时训练时,我们会建议学生背诵雅思核心词汇,以及金融、旅游、市场营销方向的专业词汇。这些材料都可以从如今丰富的网络资源上下载,关键是词汇背诵的方式,和教师检查和督促的方法。原则上,我们的带队教师会每日布置单词听写以及一些名言名句的听写,单词背诵量为每日50—100个,10句名言的程度,听写则大致20个单词和5个句子,有时也会准备生动的词汇课替代常规听写。

第二节　语言基础

除根据训练要求自编内容以外,我们还借助了《雅思核心词汇(基础篇)》《雅思核心词汇(提高篇)》《中职英语技能大赛宝典(服务类)》《中职英语技能大赛宝典(其他类)》《英语魔法师之语法俱乐部》《BEC商务英语(中级)》《Preliminary English test (PET)真题集》等书籍,为学生打造语法基础,训练阅读技巧,提升语言的综合能力。

第三节　建议训练方案

在准备技能大赛的日子里,我们除了对内容有所规划,对训练的时间、强度亦有所计划。下面是大赛前3个月及前1个月的训练建议,除此之外也建议团队的主负责人针对选手赛前一周的训练任务和表现,订定每周复习计划和训练重点,提升效率,有的放矢,从而达到事半功倍的效果。

一、未雨绸缪(长期规划,preparation> 3 months)

技能大赛前3个月训练计划				
时间	周一	周二	周三	周四	周五
8:05—8:45	新闻要点、单词听写	新闻要点、单词听写	新闻要点、单词听写	新闻要点、单词听写	新闻要点、单词听写
8:55—9:35	笔试、情景交流、职场应用(模拟训练)(真题),均录像拍摄,文稿留存并输入成电子稿	作业讲解、笔试分析	作业讲解	语法训练	自我归纳和复习
9:35—10:15			阅读训练	听力专项	20道问题解答与训练,交流重写后的回答,背诵并表演,以及快问快答
10:15—10:55					
11:05—11:35			问答部分的模板(情景)	问答部分的模板(职场)	
1:15—2:05	分析情景交流,引入词汇、句子(名言)、模板	分析职场应用,引入词汇、句子(名言)、模板	语法讲解	数字化阅读(训练)上机训练	情景交流,职场应用(自出题训练)(录像)
2:20—3:00	重新撰写情景交流,稿件输入电子稿	重新撰写职场应用,稿件输入电子稿	语法训练	针对相关领域或专题思维训练(mind map)	
3:10—3:50	观看情景交流的视频,分析问题	观看情景交流的视频,分析问题	听故事音频,找主旨大意、情感体现之处	本周同图训练情景交流、职场应用,录像并分析	录像分析
4:00—4:40	情景交流表演第二遍(录像)	职场应用第二遍(录像)	仪态训练(讲故事,给出文本)		
作业	听力、阅读2篇,背诵所教句子、词汇	听力、阅读2篇,背诵所教句子、词汇	听力、阅读2篇,背诵所教句子、词汇	听力、阅读2篇,背诵所教句子、词汇	总结归纳本周词汇、句子、模板
	情景交流5个问题的回答	职场应用5个问题的回答	情景交流类似5问重写	职场应用类似5问题	阅读2篇
		布置视频作业,模仿仪态	语法相关训练		

二、一击即中(冲刺方案,preparation<1 month)

赛前冲刺1个月				
时间	周一	周二	周三	周四	周五
8:05—8:45	新闻要点、名人名言	新闻要点、名人名言	新闻要点、名人名言	新闻要点、名人名言	新闻要点、名人名言

续 表

赛前冲刺1个月				
时间	周一	周二	周三	周四	周五
8:55—9:35	笔试、情景交流、职场应用(模拟训练)(真题),均录像拍摄,文稿留存并输入成电子稿	作业讲解和视频分析	语法混合训练	A讲图片故事(5+5);B准备回答情景交流20道题	复习本周训练重点和题目
9:35—10:15		先分析职场应用,A写稿子,B准备问题			
10:15—10:55		A、B分开训练(各自表演,录像)		欣赏优秀演讲者文本	理清相关专题思路、问题,以及词汇(专题B)
11:05—11:35				读后感与名人名言应用	再次听写
1:15—2:05	分析笔试	看辩论视频	笔试上机训练	随机进班演讲(录像)	情景交流,职场应用(自出题训练)(录像)
2:20—3:00		语言语调,归纳论点			
3:10—3:50	分析情景交流:A写稿子,B准备5道问题	分专题讲解可用到的词汇和句型(专题A)	题目分析,讲解	录像分析	录像分析
4:00—4:40	A、B分开训练(各自表演,录像)	即兴演讲小故事训练(录视频)	听写专题和辩论视频的词汇、句子	重温模板(A和B)	
作业	听力、阅读2篇,背诵所教句子、词汇	听力、阅读2篇,背诵所教句子、词汇	听力、阅读2篇,背诵所教句子、词汇	听力、阅读2篇,背诵所教句子、词汇	总结归纳本周词汇、句子、模板
	分析录像	给出5幅图片,给B10个问题	整理材料		情景交流、职场应用稿件重写,周六发
					看视频,概括视频梗概及词汇。

第六章　赛事前沿

　　2020年秋天,在原大赛大纲的基础上,宁波市职成教英语教研室又对技能大赛进行了调整与优化。新的比赛模式紧追时事和当下教育热点,我们可以从去年大赛真题中窥探一二。高一组的辩题是关于学生在课堂上使用智能手机,高二组则是中职生对实习的看法。可见去年国家提出的智能手机不能进校园和中职生要加强职业导向等已成为技能训练的重要议题。在备赛方面,选手依然以组队方式进行准备,然而区别于以往两届提前两周拿题备赛,本次又回归到现场抽题的模式。比赛现场,选手共同阅读200—300字的短文,从短文中归纳、提炼要点,展开自己的论述。准备时间为半个小时,时间结束后,A选手上台展示小组观点,B选手进行现场问答。这就更考验带队老师在平时对于语言综合能力的培养与训练,以及对热点新闻的关注与解读。

　　虽然比赛模式有所变化,但本书的笔试模拟和思维训练部分依然可以帮助学生拓宽思维,强化语言基础。原有的题型也可以作为时事热点改编的基础,为学生的演讲做准备。相信各位老师在借鉴本书备赛模式后亦能使你的训练指导上升一个台阶。

附件

Living Video Games

Many people love playing video games, no matter they are young or not. <u>Despite various kinds of video games, they are not beyond of winning or losing, living or dying, scoring points or getting destroyed. The same elements are used in game after game.</u> The figures move according to fixed patterns, make sound or short speeches, bump into obstacles, end up in tricky situations, and save themselves—or not. <u>As an introductory movement in music to playing the games in this section, talk about your favorite video games. What elements do they have in common?</u>

1. Locomotion

Props: a sound system; cartoon music

Every video game invovles movement. Characters must walk, run, jump, fall, kick, punch, leap, and son on. Not only that, each character has its own style of moving. One monster lurches around, its enormous bulk wobbling on little crooked legs. A soccer player moves quite differently than a ninja or a zombie. Invite the group to practice moving like the creatures in an imaginary video game. If you wish, have them move to suitable music. The players can move acrooss the room from corner to corner, one by one, so that everyone can see the different "walks". Encourage players to creat all kinds of different characters: not only monsters and robots, but also creatures that make supple fluid movements.

2. Emotions and sound

Many figures in video games have their emotions and they have their facial expression and sound under different conditions like laugh, grunt, scream and so on. Think about your characters' emotions and sound.

3. Obstacles and pathway

Obstacles force characters to seek out safe pathway through the game. For instance, in some situation, the character would "die" if he didn't "jump". Devise and follow an imaginary circuit around the room, complete with various obstacles and traps.

Adapted from 101 More Drama Games For Children

参考文献

［1］浙江省教育考试院.浙江省教育考试院关于发布《浙江省高校招生职业技能考试大纲》的通知[EB/OL]. http://www.zjks.net/moban/index/93806.html, 2014-04-28.

［2］浙江省教育考试院.浙江省教育考试院关于调整部分高校招生职业技能考试大纲的通知[EB/OL]. https://www.zjzs.net/moban/index/105901.html.

［3］教育部.教育部关于印发新修订的中等职业学校语文等七门公共基础课程教学大纲的通知[EB/OL]. http://www.moe.gov.cn/srcsite/A07/s7055/200901/t20090106_79143.html.

［5］教育部.关于发布中等职业学校艺术、英语等2门课程标准的公告[EB/OL]. http://www.moe.gov.cn/jyb_xxgk/s5743/s5744/A07/202003/t20200309_429184.html.

［6］Paul R. 101 More Drama Games for Children: New Fun and Learning with Acting and Make-Believe[M]. Turner Pub C., 2002.